BUSINESS
GURUS

Edited by Ian Wallis

Business Gurus

Published in Great Britain in 2012 by
Crimson Publishing Ltd
Westminster House
Kew Road
Richmond
Surrey
TW9 2ND

A catalogue record for this book is available from the British Library.

ISBN 978 1 78059 048 6

Typeset by Mac Style, Beverley, East Yorkshire
Printed and bound by in the UK by Ashford Colour Press, Gosport, Hants

Contents

Business Gurus

Foreword

Loving business and desiring to learn more about it, I always wanted to study for an MBA. However, like so many people, I became caught up in a highly successful growing business which left me no time to consider even a part-time MBA. After my first business, I almost immediately set up another, and so the MBA never happened. But with every year that passes, although I know more about business than the year before, I also know that there is more I want to know than ever. I have read material about and by a number of the business gurus featured in this book, but longed to have the time to read much more. In today's world, it seems time is our most precious commodity, and so very few of us have the time to read anywhere near as much as we would like.

This book is a great solution for me – and I hope it will prove the same for you. It is designed to summarize the key theories each guru has developed and to provide enough context and background for you to grasp the basics of them all. I would expect that everyone reading this book will want to go on to read more about or by some of the thought leaders included here; one key objective of this book, therefore, is to guide you to decide which thinkers you would like to learn more about.

The pace of change in business has picked up substantially in the last decade, with digital capabilities challenging established business models in many industries. We have included what we believe to be the best mix of classic business thinking and the best of the new wave of digital visionaries. Inevitably, we have had to exclude a number of worthy gurus.

I hope this book will prove useful to a very broad audience: from business studies students at schools and colleges, middle managers hungry to learn more, to entrepreneurs running their own business. Please do let us know what you think of *Business Gurus*. We expect to issue updated editions in the future, bringing in newer thought leaders and incorporating feedback from readers. Please email your feedback to businessgurusfeedback@ crimsonpublishing.co.uk.

We live in incredibly interesting times. The business world is changing rapidly and offers countless opportunities today, as well as countless threats. Yet, as some of the wise people featured in this book have commented, business fundamentals remain the same: it is about giving customers what they want and earning a sensible profit for doing so. I firmly believe that the classic business strategies included here remain as useful as when they were first written; when blended with the best in contemporary thinking it should lead to resounding business success.

David Lester
December 2011
London

About the authors

Mirza Aiz Baig, MBA

Mirza was awarded a Bachelor of Veterinary Science from the University of Liverpool, is a member of the Royal College of Veterinary Surgeons and has an MBA from Henley Business School. He is a commercially minded life science professional for the health care sector, with expertise in business development, team leadership and stakeholder management.

Colin Barrow, MBA, FRSA

Colin was until recently head of the Enterprise Group at Cranfield School of Management, where he taught entrepreneurship on the MBA and other programs. He is a visiting professor at business schools in the US, Asia, France, Ireland and Austria, and has been a non-executive director on a venture capital fund. He is the author of more than 20 business books including *Business Plans for Small Businesses* (published by Crimson).

Ditlev Bredahl, MBA

Ditlev is an internet and hosting veteran and the founder and CEO of OnApp, a leading provider of software for hosts. Before founding OnApp, he led UK2 Group's hosting companies as managing director and CEO, and spearheaded the launch of VPS.NET, which now operates one of the world's five largest public clouds. Ditlev has an MBA in International Business from the European Institute for Public Affairs and Lobbying in Brussels.

Gerard Burke

Gerard is the founder and MD of Your Business Your Future, the UK's leading specialist provider of development programs for ambitious owner-managers. He is a senior visiting fellow at Cass Business School in London and a high-profile speaker, writer and media commentator on owner-managers and their businesses. Gerard was previously on the faculty at Cranfield School of Management for 12 years and prior to that spent 10 years as a management consultant with PricewaterhouseCoopers.

Robert Craven

Robert is a best-selling author, entrepreneur and managing director of The Directors' Centre. He shows ambitious business directors how to run significantly more successful businesses. The 'UK's #1 speaker" (speakermix.com), Robert delivers consulting work for, and is a personal mentor to, the leaders of a number of growing businesses in the UK. He is the author of *Grow Your Service Firm* and *Bright Marketing* (both published by Crimson).

Christopher Fung

Christopher is the managing director of Crussh, the UK's leading healthy eating chain, serving juices, smoothies and fit food in 26 sites across Central London. An ex-Bain & Co consultant, he is responsible for the overall direction of the company, and ensuring the success of the growth plan. In the past few years he has overseen the turnaround of the business and the building of the Crussh brand as it stands today, as well as setting the vision for their range of food and drinks.

Clive Hemingway, MBA

Clive has worked in academic publishing since 1982, and has witnessed the many industry changes brought about by the internet. His experience includes periods with multinationals (Thomson, Elsevier), SMEs and non-profit organizations, primarily in editorial roles, but also in marketing, production and IT. In 2011, he gained an MBA from Henley Business School.

Trudi Knight, MBA

Trudi relocated to the UK in 1997 after working for Nestlé in New Zealand. She is an accomplished business finance executive with more than 15 years' experience across FMCG, media, IT and financial services sectors. Along with her work in finance, she has completed a number of strategic evaluation projects. Most recently, Trudi was awarded an MBA from Henley Business School.

Jeremy Lazarus

Jeremy is a certified Master Trainer of NLP, as well as a business performance coach, and has over 25 years' business experience. He runs his own NLP training company in London, training people to harness the power of NLP in business and sport. His clients range from blue chip companies to elite, Olympic athletes. He has written three books, including the Amazon number 1 best-seller *Successful NLP* (published by Crimson).

David Lester

David qualified as a chartered accountant before becoming a successful entrepreneur. He started his first business at the age of 22, which he built into a highly profitable company before selling it in 1995 to a Nasdaq-listed company. He then founded Crimson Publishing, publishers of this book and the UK's most popular small business websites Startups.co.uk, MyBusiness.co.uk and GrowingBusiness.co.uk.

John Maxted

John is an entrepreneur who founded Digby Morgan, the leading international HR recruitment company, acquired by Randstad in February 2011. He resigned as CEO following the sale of the business and is now actively involved in the charity sector, politics and working with private companies as an adviser, investor and non-executive director.

Dominic Monkhouse, MBA

Dominic is the managing director of PEER 1 Hosting's EMEA operations. He has spent 15 years working in sales, marketing and business management within the IT sector. Prior to joining PEER 1 Hosting, he held senior positions at IT Lab and Rackspace. Dominic has a BSc in Agricultural and Food Marketing from Newcastle and an MBA from Sheffield Business School. Dominic is also a regular public speaker and an assessor on the *Sunday Times* Customer Experience Awards.

Lara Morgan

Lara is the founder of CompanyShortcuts.com and author of the Amazon best-seller *More Balls than Most*. She is a straight-talking entrepreneur who understands the frustrations felt by small and medium-sized businesses that have lost their way. Lara built her own international business, Pacific Direct, before selling a majority share 99% holding of the company for £20m in 2008. With a passion for learning intact, she now strives to support entrepreneurs who want to maximize success.

Modwenna Rees-Mogg

Modwenna is the author of *Dragons or Angels*, the unofficial guide to *Dragons' Den* and a handbook for people wanting to become or raise money from business angels. She owns and operates AngelNews, a media business focused on business angels, VCs and early stage-funded companies. Prior to founding AngelNews, Modwenna ran an angel group and has been an angel investor. She started her career as a corporate financier at Kleinwort Benson.

Clive Rich

Clive is the UK's leading deal-maker and trouble-shooter, and has played a crucial role brokering more than £10bn worth of deals for a broad spectrum of multinationals, major organizations and super-brands including Sony, Yahoo, Apple, Napster, BMG and the BBC. An Oxford University and the Inns of Court Law graduate, Clive has more than 25 years' experience creating and closing deals.

Mark Roy

Mark is founder and CEO of The REaD Group plc and chair of the Direct Marketing Association's Data Council. Early in his career, he had spells in the publishing and travel sectors. In 1991, he started The REaD Group with £25,000 of his own money and the company has since grown to become one of the largest and most influential in direct marketing. Twenty years on and Mark has become a well-known and respected figure within the industry.

Andrew J Scott

Andrew is a serial entrepreneur. After creating an irreverent magazine at school, he set up an IT consultancy with his college as his first client. Some of his internet start-ups include a web development company, the world's first online digital video news archive (British Pathe), an interactive fitness website (Intraining), the world's first location-based mobile social network (Playtxt) and a personalization company (Rummble). Today, Andrew consults and advises tech start-ups and is on the board of founder group ICE.

Kate Walters

Kate has been writing for publications including Startups. co.uk and *Growing Business* since 2006. She is currently editor of Growingbusiness.co.uk and has interviewed dozens of entrepreneurs and business leaders with a focus on their start-up stories and growth strategies. She graduated from Warwick University in 2005 with a degree in Philosophy and Literature.

Acknowledgements

The existence of *Business Gurus* is due in a very large part to its esteemed contributing authors. Conceived by David Lester as a pocket-sized MBA, the title distils 28 of the world's best and foremost business thinkers and their seminal theories into one book.

Uniquely, *Business Gurus* has been written by an assembly of authors intimately acquainted with their subjects' work. And unlike other such titles, the book approaches each guru and their works from the business practitioners' point of view, seeking to understand how the gurus' theories are applied in real business environments.

We sought a variety of experienced and knowledgeable authors, namely entrepreneurs that have been influenced by a particular guru(s), business school professors and business program leaders, MBAs, and also an experienced business journalist. In total, 18 authors contributed the 28 chapters of this book and are due my sincere gratitude for the time and effort they put in to their respective chapters.

In addition, I would like to thank GrowingBusiness.co.uk's editor Kate Walters for commissioning the chapters written by Ditlev Bredahl, Dominic Monkhouse and Clive Rich, as well as writing her own chapter. Crimson's Gareth Platt is also worthy of considerable appreciation for his assistance in editing two of the chapters.

I would also like to thank Clive Hemingway, who authored a chapter and acted as an editorial consultant, utilising his impressive knowledge of his chosen gurus' works. And finally, there are a considerable number of people at Crimson who have helped to make sure *Business Gurus* was published.

Chris Anderson

By Robert Craven

Name: Chris Anderson

Born: 1961

Expertise: Technology journalism and commentary on the evolution of our digital world

Known for: Editorship of *Wired* magazine; advocating that companies should focus on niche markets

Best-known titles: *The Long Tail: Why the Future of Business is Selling Less of More* (2006); *Free: The Future of a Radical Price* (2009)

Who is Chris Anderson?

Chris Anderson started his professional career as a research physicist, before moving into science journalism with *Nature* and *Science*. He then worked for *The Economist* in a number of positions including technology editor and US business editor before taking over the editorship of *Wired* in 2001. His books have both been bestsellers. His interests include music and robotics.

What is Anderson known for?

The phrase 'the long tail' derived from an article by Clay Shirky. Essays by Anderson published in *Wired* culminated in *The Long Tail* book in 2006. The long tail concept showed that the traditional blockbuster/bestseller/hits model would become less ubiquitous as the price of manufacture, distribution, storage of products was combined with increasingly powerful intermediaries and opinion-formers.

The argument explained the growth of businesses such as Amazon, Netflix and countless specialist niche businesses (often small or privately owned) in the internet age. This was in a world where everyone was still making it up as they went along – no-one knew what the next big thing in the internet would be or why. More importantly, there was a struggle to understand how big players and small players were to make money from the new technology.

In a world where rapidly changing technologies make the world more connected and interconnected, *The Long Tail* was the first book to explain exactly how the ability to reach niche markets would create big opportunities.

The concepts

In a nutshell, *The Long Tail* examines how the economy (and culture) is increasingly shifting away from the bestsellers, so from a relatively small numbers of 'hits', at the head of a demand curve and towards a huge number of niches in the tail.

The Long Tail is about the consequences of how western economies and cultures in particular are shifting from mass markets to millions of niches. It records the effect of the technologies that have made it easier for consumers to find and buy niche products. This is all thanks to the 'infinite shelf-space effect' and the new distribution mechanisms (from digital downloading to peer-to-peer markets) that break through the traditional bottlenecks of broadcast and bricks-and-mortar retail.

As the cost of production and distribution crashes, especially in the online world, there is now less need to treat consumers as one homogenous group. Without the old constraints of limited shelf space and without the old bottlenecks of distribution, narrowly targeted goods and services can thrive and be as attractive as, or even more attractive than, the mainstream hits.

Traditional retail economies can only stock a limited number of products on expensive and limited shelf space; they stock the likely hits and bestsellers to maximize stock turnaround and sales. Online retailers, on the other hand, can stock just about everything and the number of niche offerings available can outnumber the mainstream hits. In the past, these millions of niches of the long tail had largely been neglected in favor of the small number of bigger hits.

The theory in summary

1. The true shape of demand has been disguised by the limited short tail of hits that retailers were prepared to promote. However, when consumers have infinite choice the true shape of the demand curve is revealed; it turns out to be less hit-centric than previously believed. People will gravitate towards niches because they better satisfy their narrow interests.

2. The cost of reaching niches is falling dramatically thanks to a combination of forces including digital distribution, search technologies and broadband penetration. So, it is now possible to offer a far greater range of products.

3. Simply offering a greater variety does not shift demand. Consumers must be able to find the niche that suits them. Tools such as recommendations and rankings, referred to as 'filters', can drive demand down the tail.

4. Once there is massively expanded variety (and filters are in place) then the demand curve flattens – the hits are still there but they become relatively less popular (as the niches become relatively more popular).

5. All the niches add up – and collectively they can compete with the hits.

6. At this point the natural shape of the undistorted demand curve is revealed – undistorted by bottlenecks, scarcity of information and limited shelf space. A far less hit-driven demand reveals itself.

In virtually all markets there are far more niche products than hits, and the ratio is growing exponentially as the tools of production become cheaper and more readily available.

Anderson describes the three forces of the long tail as 'make it, get it out there, and help me find it'.

1. Democratizing the costs of production: toolmakers and producers (e.g. digital video, desktop music, video editing, blogging tools) become mostly free or virtually free.
2. Democratizing the costs of distribution: aggregators emerge (e.g. Amazon, eBay, iTunes, Trip Advisor).
3. Connecting supply and demand: filters (e.g. Google, blogs, recommendations and bestseller lists).

Anderson looked at retailers in movies, music and books and asked the following.

1. What is the size of the long tail (defined as inventory not available offline)?
2. How does the availability of so many niche products change the shape of demand? Does it shift away from the hits?
3. What tools and techniques drive the shift and what are the most effective?

How real companies use Anderson's concept

Anderson cites earlier research by Brynjolfsson, Hu and Smith that showed that a significant portion of Amazon.com's sales came from obscure books that are not available in bricks-and-mortar shops.

Hits tend to have relatively low profit margins because of the high set-up costs and their high failure rate. Hits tend to be sold at discounts because of the competitive nature of retailers chasing the consumer dollar. Niches, on the other hand, can be sold at full price – partially because of their scarcity. As an example, retailers might sell the latest Harry Potter book as a loss leader but sell other less-known books at full price. It is conceivable that they make more from low unit sales of a relatively unknown author (at a high profit per unit) than from the big hit sold at a loss.

Long tail aggregators (Netflix, Amazon, iTunes) often dominate their category. Of course the long tail isn't just found in media and entertainment. Think about eBay (the long tail of physical goods) or Google (the long tail of advertising), Grameen Bank (the long tail of banking).

How it dovetails with other guru theories

Anderson argues that the long tail signals the death as we know it of the Pareto principle or 80/20 rule – while the 80/20 rule implies that all focus should be on the 20% of products that generate 80% of sales revenues, *The Long Tail* suggests that there is plenty of opportunity, maybe more, in the long tail.

The Long Tail is subsequently quoted by many contemporary commentators on the internet age: Tom Peters and Seth Godin are great fans as are Nassim Nicholas Taleb in *The Black Swan*, Clay Shirky in *Here Comes Everybody*, Malcolm Gladwell in *The Tipping Point*, and the concept is used to explain and justify the focus on the importance of small niche players.

Validity today

The book is as relevant today as when it was written. It should be noted that the long tail concept is often misunderstood (like the 80/20 rule) and hence quoted out of context. Many new entrepreneurial businesses are now emerging and taking advantage of the collapse of production, storage and distribution costs alongside the increasing power of aggregators and filters. Anderson identified this new world and gave it a name. Small businesses can take advantage of it and larger businesses have to adjust their strategies to recognize that the old models are no longer as effective as they once were. It will never be 1998 again!

Igor Ansoff

By Gerard Burke

Name: Igor Ansoff

Born: 1918; **died:** 2002

Expertise: Celebrated as the pioneer of strategic management, Ansoff was the first management guru to recognize the need for strategic planning

Known for: His product-market growth matrix, which was first published in the *Harvard Business Review* (1957) in an article called 'Strategies for Diversification'. The tool is used by marketers to consider different growth strategies

Best-known titles: *Strategic Management Classic Edition* (2007); *Corporate Strategy* (1965)

Who is Igor Ansoff?

A Russian-American, applied mathematician and business manager, Ansoff is known as the father of strategic management.

Author of more than 120 published papers and articles translated in eight languages, Ansoff leads the field in applying strategic thinking to businesses, bridging the gap between concepts and practice.

Besides his academic work, Ansoff founded Ansoff Associates International with the mission of helping companies worldwide to grow profitably. The firm has provided consultancy to hundreds of multinationals including Philips, General Electric, Gulf, IBM, Sterling Europa, Westinghouse and KBB in the Netherlands.

What is Ansoff known for?

He is acclaimed for his research in three specific areas: the concept of environmental turbulence, the contingent strategic success paradigm and real-time strategic management.

His product-market growth matrix was first published in the *Harvard Business Review* (1957) in an article called 'Strategies for Diversification' and subsequently in his book on 'Corporate Strategy' in 1965 and has since become a cornerstone of marketing thinking. The matrix (see figure over the page) portrays several different business growth strategies, and can be used as a tool for deciding where to concentrate growth efforts.

Ansoff's matrix

Markets

	Existing	New
Existing **Products/** **services**	**Business Development**	**Market Development**
New	**Product Development**	**Diversification**

Pillar 5: Stick to the knitting – and stand out from the crowd

Markets

	Existing	New
Existing **Products/** **services**	**Business Development** **88%!**	**Market Development**
New	**Product Development**	**Diversification**

Nearly 90% of successful growth businesses achieve their growth by selling more of their existing products and services to their existing customers and people just like them

The concepts

Ansoff's matrix gives four possible growth strategies.

1. **Market penetration:** increasing your market share by selling more of your existing products or services to your existing customers.
2. **Market development:** selling your existing products or services into new markets.
3. **Product development:** developing new products or services targeted at your existing customers.
4. **Diversification:** developing new products or services for new markets.

Selecting a growth strategy

Market penetration

The market penetration strategy is the least risky, least costly approach as it leverages a firm's existing resources and capabilities. The further you stray away from what you know, the more risky it becomes.

Several studies in recent years make a convincing case for this argument. One study ('Innovation types and performance in growing UK SMEs' by Adegoke Oke, Arizona State University, Phoenix, US, Gerard Burke, Your Business Your Future, UK, and Andrew Myers, AJM Associates, UK), for example, found that high-performing firms showing consistently profitable growth focused on selling existing products and services to the market they already knew. In other words, they 'stuck to the knitting'.

Putting this into practice is normally a two-stage process: sell more to existing customers and then look to capture customers from your competitors.

Think of it like squeezing a lemon. When a recipe calls for the juice of half a lemon, most people will slice a lemon in two, squeeze one half and then throw away the rest. Put simply, most people will fail to get the maximum juice out of the lemon. Many businesses take exactly the same approach with their customers. There is no plan for developing the sales relationship with larger customers, no plan to encourage smaller customers to become larger ones, and no plan for finding new customers.

Squeezing the lemon – in other words, extracting the maximum value from your juiciest customers – is all about getting close to your customers; it's about knowing your customers and their businesses so well that you can anticipate what they might need from you.

'Squeezing the lemon' tactics include cross-selling, up-selling, increasing the usage rate, winning a bigger share of your customers' spend on your products/services and asking for referrals. All of these tactics depend on identifying and truly understanding the specific set of customers to whom your product/service delivers distinctive benefits. If these customers value something about your product/service that they can't get from someone else, they will be prepared to pay for your products/services, thus enabling you to avoid competing on price and maintain good margins.

Of course, market penetration has its limits and once the market approaches saturation, another strategy must be pursued if the business is to continue to grow.

Market development

Market development options include entering new market segments or geographical regions. This may be a good strategy if an organization's core competencies are related to its product rather than its experience in a specific market segment or if a firm has fully exploited its existing market.

Go Ape, the forest adventure course, is a good example of a business that has grown successfully by 'sticking to the knitting', and only looked to market development as a growth strategy once it had fully exploited its existing market.

Founded by Tristram Mayhew, Go Ape has featured in the FastTrack 100 list of the UK's 100 fastest-growing independently owned businesses for three consecutive years and won many awards including the Small-Medium Sized Business of the Year at the National Business Awards.

Mayhew opened the first Go Ape site in Thetford, UK, in 2002, and spent the next seven years setting up high-rope adventure courses in forest locations throughout the UK to the point where he says he and his team could 'roll out Go Ape courses in our sleep'. This aggressive market development strategy has meant that despite the emergence of several competitors, Go Ape's success has continued almost unabated. Profits hit £1m in 2009, and have remained in seven figures ever since, while the staff roster has increased to 450.

However, the UK naturally poses some limitations in terms of the number of Go Ape sites he can feasibly open. So in early 2009, drawing on the knowledge and experience gained from the UK, Mayhew set out to spread the Go Ape message Stateside. He mitigated the risk of entering a new territory by forming a joint venture with a US firm.

The first American site was opened in 2009 and is already proving successful, and Mayhew says he's planning on opening five or six more sites in America.

Product development

Although innovation, or investing in new products, is a higher-risk strategy than market development, there are ways to manage the risks involved. The least risky innovation is likely to be the new product or service requested by existing customers.

Continuing the Go Ape example, besides moving into new markets, Go Ape has also taken its first step outside its core tree-top climbing operation by developing products for visitors who don't want to or can't take part in the tree-top courses. Mayhew has purchased a fleet of Segway scooters for visitors to use on the forest floor, and mountain bikes are now being provided for those who prefer to stay grounded.

This type of incremental innovation, based on deep sensitivity to customers' needs, is usually a natural and deeply engrained behavior within businesses that have an ongoing focus on identifying new and better ways to service customers. Their deep knowledge of their niche allows them to respond quickly to, or even anticipate, their customers' needs. As a result, they can be seen to be constantly enhancing their products and services in ways they already know will meet with their customers' approval.

There are also several other situations in which a product development strategy may be appropriate. If a firm's strengths are related to specific customers rather than a specific product, it can leverage this strength by developing a new product targeted at existing customers.

Another reason to pursue a product development strategy is when a firm's core market becomes obsolete, perhaps due to advancements in technology. For example, Guardian News & Media, publisher of the *Guardian*, recently revealed plans to become a 'digital-first' organization, placing open journalism on the web at the heart of its strategy in the face of declining print sales.

Diversification

Diversification is a high-risk strategy. In fact, this quadrant of the matrix has been referred to as the 'suicide cell' or the 'wally box'.

Ultimately, it boils down to 'selling stuff you don't know to people you've never met', which sounds like – and often is – an impossible task.

Many business owners – because they are entrepreneurially minded – find it hard to resist the temptation of diversifying. This might seem the most dynamic route for driving a business forward, but experience and common sense suggest it's usually the highest-risk approach and rarely the most profitable.

Of course, high-performing businesses also occasionally diversify. But, radical innovation and diversification is only undertaken once the foundations have been well laid within the core niche, and as part of a carefully thought through strategy.

For example, Pacific Direct, a supplier of luxury branded toiletries, built a strong position in hotels before moving to servicing airlines. Business and first class airline passengers also tend to stay in five star hotels and appreciate the same sort of luxury brands. Pacific Direct's credentials built in one niche bolstered its entry into the adjacent one and the company's infrastructure was robust enough to support the expansion.

How real companies use Ansoff's concepts

Pillinger Controls, a Surrey-based firm that designs energy-management systems for commercial premises, has recently discovered the benefits of 'sticking to the knitting'. The company had grown quite significantly in the seven years since it was created; the workforce had swelled from four to 40, and turnover had hit £3m. However, rather than growing up gracefully, the company had, in director Mike Darby's own words, 'got big in a badly managed fashion'. Turnover had gone up but profitability had fallen, and the company was starting to lose staff.

The root of the problem was that Pillinger wasn't being discerning about who its customers were. It was selling to people who were not part of the set of customers who really valued the benefits its service delivered.

The majority of Pillinger's business was coming from building contractors who were working on projects where architects or others had specified installation of an energy-management system for controlling heating, ventilation and air conditioning. For the building contractors, the installation of the energy-management system was purely a box-ticking exercise, rather than work to minimize energy consumption and reduce the lifetime running costs of a building.

Essentially, Pillinger was selling to customers who didn't value its product, and it started to take its toll; cash flow had become a nightmare because of the payment terms in the contracting world and because customers would try to beat them down on price. This wasn't doing Pillinger's reputation any good and it was crippling morale.

The company took the difficult decision to stop working with contractors and instead focus on the market that really valued its service – accountancy firms, banks and public sector organizations who own and occupy large portfolios of buildings. These organizations are actually interested in getting more value out of their systems, which is exactly where Pillinger's strength lies.

Having identified its niche, Pillinger is now looking to exploit it by 'squeezing the lemon' – in other words, extracting the maximum value from its 'juiciest' customers. The time it was wasting on contracting jobs is now spent on nurturing relationships with owner-occupier customers.

How it dovetails with other guru theories

The concept of a planning gap analysis has been developed by several researchers. This builds on Ansoff's growth strategies by pitching the anticipated result of each growth strategy against a desired strategic outcome. Managers can then see how large the gap is (if any) between the desired outcome and the results of pursuing a strategy. It also informs managers about the level of risk involved in closing any gap, stemming typically from the amount of change required. The result of a planning gap analysis may require some moderation of the desired outcomes if strategic leaders are not content with the amount of risk entailed in closing the gap.

Another technique for forward business planning is 'scenario planning'. While Ansoff takes account of external environmental factors, scenario planning looks harder at how those factors might plausibly interact to affect a strategic outcome.

Validity today

As the examples above demonstrate, Ansoff's matrix and the message of 'sticking to the knitting' is just as relevant today as it was 50 years ago. In fact, in many ways it's more important. We are currently going through one of the most turbulent times in economic history, and not all businesses will survive the storm. In the current climate, many companies will try to compete on price. Usually this is because they don't have a distinctive benefit so they make price their point of difference. The key to 'sticking to the knitting' is identifying your distinctiveness and targeting customers who value and are willing to pay for this benefit. Businesses that have something distinctive that customers are prepared to pay for won't need to get drawn into price wars and can protect their profit margins.

So the message is: go deep, before going broad. Entering new markets and developing innovative new products/services may well play an important role at certain specific stages of growth, but only at the right time and only as part of an overall strategy.

Richard Bandler and John Grinder

By Jeremy Lazarus

Names: Richard Wayne Bandler and John Thomas Grinder

Born: Bandler 1950; Grinder 1940

Expertise: Neurolinguistic programming (NLP)

Known for: Bandler and Grinder were the co-creators of NLP

Best-known titles: *Frogs Into Princes: The Introduction to Neuro-Linguistic Programming* (1979); *The Structure of Magic: A Book About Language & Therapy* (1975); *The Structure of Magic II: A Book About Communication and Change* (1975)

Who are Richard Bandler and John Grinder?

As co-creators of neurolinguistic programming (NLP) in the 1970s, Bandler and Grinder have made major contributions to the field of personal development and personal excellence. These two aspects are designed to benefit people in their life generally, and have extensive applications in the workplace. In the 1970s Grinder was an associate professor of linguistics at University of California at Santa Cruz; Bandler studied philosophy and psychology.

What are Bandler and Grinder known for?

Their early books and ideas concentrated on linguistics and communication. Based on their studies of the work of eminent figures around that time from the worlds of therapy, linguistics and anthropology, such as Virginia Satir, Fritz Perls, Milton Erickson MD, Noam Chomsky, Gregory Bateson and others, they developed ideas about how individuals could change their own thinking and responses to situations, and how 'therapists' could communicate effectively to assist this.

Bandler and Grinder ran seminars and practice groups regarding their work, and in 1979 published their seminal work on NLP, *Frogs into Princes*. The book has three main chapters and subject areas, although there are several NLP topics and techniques in the book. Since then they have written numerous books both together and separately; the field of NLP and range of 'techniques' have expanded greatly, to the point where NLP is used in practically every field of human endeavor, not merely in personal development. NLP centers around attempting to help people create changes in all aspects of their life (including work) so that they can have more of what they want and less of what they don't want. There are three key strands to NLP.

1. **To improve communication:** both with other people and the way we communicate with ourselves (for example, 'negative' self-talk).
2. **To help people change behaviors and ways of thinking:** be they relatively superficial, such as being calm instead of nervous when giving a business presentation and thinking that the audience will be interested rather than bored, through to deeper behaviors and thinking patterns that may have significant negative consequences.
3. **To provide a methodology to model excellence:** so that an individual's excellence at performing a skill (such as closing a sale, trading foreign exchange or motivating staff) can be replicated.

Given these applications, it is hardly surprising that NLP is applicable in any area where people operate and have relationships, such as the workplace, sport, healthcare, education, coaching and therapy. Indeed, NLP is included on many soft-skills training courses even if they are not referred to as NLP.

The concepts

The focus of many senior business executives is on profits, shareholder value, systems, processes and strategies, and important as all these are, none of this can be achieved without the engagement of the workforce. Almost all annual reports and accounts will make reference to the importance of the employees in the chairman's or chief executive's statement. The success of any business will depend to a large degree on the relationships it forms with internal and external stakeholders, and the personal effectiveness of its staff.

This section will consider the business applications of NLP, and how it is used in the workplace. The three NLP strands outlined above are capable of having an impact on the 15 essential business activities (this list is not exhaustive):

- selling
- procuring
- managing staff, including staff motivation/engagement and coaching
- advertising
- recruiting
- interviewing
- negotiating
- presenting
- team-building
- strategic planning
- training
- conflict prevention and/or resolution
- business process improvement
- product creation
- having effective meetings.

Let's now look at some specific NLP concepts and techniques that are used within the business activities above. It is important to make the following clear before we proceed.

- Because NLP was developed by modelling excellence, it is completely possible that an individual or a group may be using some of the concepts below without having been trained in NLP.

- Some people question whether it is appropriate to use the powerful NLP communication skills. Remember, people communicate anyway, and so it is probably more useful to do so in a way that gives you more chance to achieve your desired outcome, and ideally to create win-win situations.
- Each concept is covered only very briefly. Whole chapters in books and segments of training courses are devoted to how to use each individual concept.

Underpinning beliefs: the mindset for success

Those working effectively within the field of NLP use a series of beliefs, known as 'pre-suppositions', in their work. These are assumptions which, when we act as if they are true, will help facilitate better results, faster. Typically there are around 15 pre-suppositions.

One such pre-supposition is, 'there is no failure, only feedback'. If we do not achieve the desired results in an activity (for example a sales pitch), treating it as a failure will probably lead to some form of unhelpful negativity (often found in 'blame cultures'), whereas treating it purely as feedback creates a mindset for learning and developing and hence increases the likelihood of future success.

Another pre-supposition is that the more flexible we can be (as individuals or as a business), the more likely we are to succeed.

Rapport

'Rapport' can be defined as a spirit of trust and cooperation between two or more people. People can build rapport by the processes of 'matching' or 'mirroring' body language, voice and certain aspects of language. It underpins virtually all successful relationships, including the 15 business aspects listed earlier, particularly selling, managing, procuring, interviewing, presenting and negotiating. Almost everyone automatically builds rapport with their friends. All NLP books and training courses will cover 'rapport'.

Seeing other perspectives

Known as 'perceptual positions', being able to put oneself in someone else's shoes, or to consider different perspectives, is invaluable in business, for example, when preparing for a meeting (sales, interview, appraisal, negotiation) or presentation, or if there is a conflict. When planning strategy, perceptual positions can help consider the position of various stakeholders, or the likely outcomes of different strategic options.

Language and questions

Arguably Bandler and Grinder are best known for this aspect, and they developed several models and aspects of language which are used in business. Given that whenever we speak or write we are communicating, our choice of words can subtly (and sometimes not so subtly) influence others. Here is a simple example. Assuming a salesperson wants to build good relationships with clients, saying, 'I agree, *but* ... ' is probably not as effective as saying, 'I agree, *and* ...'. More generally, the quality of the questions we ask will have an impact on the quality of our outcomes. Asking, 'How, specifically, are we going to do task X?' may be really useful, but if we haven't already asked, 'What is the purpose/benefit of task X? Is it in line with our overall strategy?', it might not be. As some NLP trainers say: 'Many people try to get to the top of the ladder as fast as they can without first asking whether the ladder is against the right wall.'

Being in the right state

Based on work done by Pavlov, there is a technique in NLP (called 'anchoring') which helps people to feel at their best and in a resourceful state, for example confident, calm, motivated. This can be extremely useful when selling, negotiating, presenting or at interviews.

What's important to you?

This is possibly the most useful of the NLP topics for managing, engaging and getting the best from people, and is known in NLP as 'values'. If every manager took the time to find out what was truly important to every member of his/her staff and what they really wanted from the job, and then took action (within the existing constraints of the business) to help each member of staff have what was important to them, the likelihood is that staff would feel significantly more engaged, and less likely to want to leave. 'Values' also has potential benefits when selling, since prospective clients would be more likely to buy if their needs were understood and met.

How real companies use Bandler and Grinder's concepts

Most training courses that involve personal effectiveness, management and leadership skills, influencing skills or selling will have a significant component of NLP communication skills, whether or not it is labeled as NLP. Hundreds, if not thousands, of UK companies sponsor staff to attend NLP courses and/or provide in-house NLP-based training each year.

Many trained business coaches use NLP techniques to help clients change their behaviors, beliefs and ways of thinking. One

NLP colleague alone has coached and trained senior managers and directors in more than half of the FTSE-100 companies.

Another colleague has assisted a large construction company to win more tender contracts by changing some of the language it used in its proposals. And another, when she was head of HR at a blue chip manufacturing company, used the 'perceptual positions' technique to resolve a sexual harassment complaint brought against a director, and the whole process lasted less than two hours. One shudders to think of the cost (both legal fees and the company's reputation) had this been taken to court.

Norwegian mineral water producer Isklar had an advertising campaign in the UK in 2008, where it used language that linked to readers' sensory experience. In NLP, these are known as 'predicates' and 'representational systems'. The author has no knowledge of whether the creators of the adverts intentionally used NLP.

How it dovetails with other guru theories

Bandler and Grinder created NLP by modeling the work of Virginia Satir, Fritz Perls, Milton Erickson MD, Noam Chomsky, Gregory Bateson and others. Given that a significant part of NLP is about modeling excellence, there will be aspects of NLP that dovetail with other leading theories. For example, one of the NLP pre-suppositions is that it is useful to respect other people's points of view, regardless of whether we agree with them. This seems to link to one of Stephen Covey's 'seven habits' – 'seek first to understand, then to be understood'.

Another aspect of NLP is the area of goal-setting, whereby if we set goals that meet certain criteria they are said to be 'well-formed goals' and hence more likely to be achieved. Many people in business are aware of the SMART goal acronym (specific, measureable, achievable, realistic and timed), and the approach to creating a 'well-formed' goal takes this significantly further. In addition, setting well-formed goals links to the work of Napoleon Hill (*Think and Grow Rich*). Hill stresses the importance of people having a compelling goal that they have already seen achieved in detail in their mind.

Hill developed his knowledge and approaches by, in effect, modeling high achievers in the world of business. Whether or not Bandler and Grinder were influenced by Hill's work, they too used modeling to develop their theories and practices around human excellence.

One of the aspects that set Bandler and Grinder's work apart from, for example, Hill's and Covey's, is that it provides a selection of specific techniques to change one's mindset, normally quickly and with lasting effects.

Validity today

As mentioned earlier, NLP is taught and used within businesses and the workplace daily. Many training courses and business trainers incorporate NLP. From its beginnings in the mid-1970s, NLP has developed to the extent that some UK universities have recognized NLP training as part of certain coaching-based master's degrees.

As one might expect, Bandler and Grinder continue to develop their theories. Although they no longer work together, Grinder has developed 'New Code' NLP, and Bandler has developed Design Human Engineering™, both of which expand on their original work.

Ken Blanchard

By Lara Morgan

Name: Ken Blanchard

Born: 1939

Expertise: Global authority on leadership, in particular the day-to-day management of people and companies. Currently a trustee emeritus at Cornell University, and visiting professor at the Cornell University School of Hotel Administration

Known for: Blanchard is one of the world's most prolific leadership and management authors, having written more than 30 books on the subject

Best-known titles: *The One Minute Manager* (1982); *Raving Fans: A Revolutionary Approach to Customer Service* (1993); *Gung Ho! Turn On the People in Any Organization* (1998)

Who is Ken Blanchard?

Born in New Jersey and raised in New York, Blanchard holds a master's degree from Colgate University, and a PhD from Cornell University.

Few people have devoted more time and ink to the concept of leadership than Ken Blanchard. In addition to running his own company, which specializes in training and workplace productivity, and speaking at countless events around the world, Blanchard has written more than 30 books on the principles of leadership, and his quick, simple prose has attracted millions of devoted followers.

Blanchard believes that positive, personal relationships between management and staff lie at the core of every organization, and he has championed this approach relentlessly through his work – most famously in *The One Minute Manager*, his biggest-selling book.

What is Blanchard known for?

Although Blanchard has written a number of books in partnership with other authors, he is most famous for the 'One Minute' series – a family of short, sharp management bibles which have brought huge commercial success.

The One Minute Manager, written in partnership with Spencer Johnson, has sold more than 12 million copies; readers across the world have been drawn in by his formula for managerial success, based on quick, proactive treatment of staff and personal communication with all levels of the organization. Meanwhile the *One Minute Entrepreneur* offers solutions to a plethora of everyday business problems, and the *One Minute Apology* offers tips in repairing business relationships with honesty and openness.

Blanchard's literary success owes much to his concise approach to management; his books are short, the font is large and the concepts are simplified with allegories, providing an engaging human focus. The simplistic and accessible style of the books makes them highly appealing to travelers looking for quick-to-action new skills and habits that get immediate results. The format of his books is also ideal for managers looking to continually apply progress and refresh their own skills and leadership abilities. His priceless stories play a crucial role in re-energizing, invigorating and reminding tired managers how to get the best from their teams.

Humor plays a part in the simplicity of Blanchard's intentionally easy-flowing conversational approach, but do not expect anything other than big results if you apply lessons learnt well. In *The One Minute Manager*, the journey his invented, yet very real, learning manager takes is intelligently realistic and everyday conversations have impact through Blanchard's creation of life-like situations which everyone can understand and appreciate.

These life-like situations, based on everyday office scenarios, provide clear lessons in the way our approach impacts on others; what we say, how we say it and when we say it has a huge impact on our staff. In *The One Minute Manager*, Blanchard uses a series of key thinking messages to show how, by thinking more broadly and putting people at the heart of the company, we can gain extraordinary results – often in adverse situations. The example conversations Blanchard writes give us simple and easy-to-apply leadership skills and conversations to enact with the clear objective of making every workplace engagement more enjoyable and more profitable.

The concepts

Blanchard's theory on management, espoused in *The One Minute Manager*, is predicated on the notion of servant leadership, whereby managers allow their staff to take key functions and decisions into their own hands, building up their individual skill-sets while enhancing the company as a collective. Blanchard's approach can be summed up in two of his most famous statements: that 'the key to successful leadership today is influence, not authority', and 'too many leaders act as if the sheep ... their people ... are there for the benefit of the shepherd, not that the shepherd has responsibility for the sheep'.

To empower staff, Blanchard recommends that managers deal with each employee clearly and consistently; he advocates a 'philosophy of no surprises', which requires the manager to be crystal clear in both their praise and constructive criticism.

Blanchard's formula for successful management also advocates speed and simplicity. The speedier, and more specific, a manager can be in responding to his staffs' achievements, the more they will value his input. Indeed *The One Minute Manager* preaches the idea that key management functions should take no longer than a minute.

The key functions outlined in *The One Minute Manager* are as follows.

- **One-minute goal setting:** managers should help their staff set a series of objectives by which to measure future performance. Each goal should take no more than 250 words to explain, and the overall list of goals should cover no more than a page. Anyone should be able to read the full list within a minute.

- **One-minute praising:** during the early stages of an employee's spell with the company, the manager should monitor their work and respond quickly whenever they do something worthy of praise. The praising session should take no longer than a minute, and the manager should take care to explain exactly what the employee has done well – leaving no room for doubt.
- **One-minute reprimanding:** just like the praising, the reprimand has to be clear and unambiguous, taking no more than a minute. The employee must be left in no doubt as to where they've gone wrong, and the manager must also make clear that, despite their aberration, the employee is highly valued within the company.

These one-minute skills are designed to ensure that individuals feel valued, focused and involved in the overall business performance. Ultimately, according to Blanchard, staff should be able to take ownership of these skills – enhancing their own performance and employability, while giving the manager more free time.

Blanchard's blueprint also demands continuous self-monitoring and a rigorous desire for enhancement. Indeed his books are filled with superb take-away checklists, which if relentlessly shared, applied and reviewed, ensure habit-changing performance improvement throughout the organization. Ultimately, Blanchard expects us to share the same experiences and learning effort with those around us for far-reaching improvements and to build a momentum of success at the core of the company's culture.

How real companies use Blanchard's concepts

In companies with great leadership and solid cultural foundations, where every individual feels part of the team and engaged in the success of the business, the examples of *The One Minute Manager* are played out every hour. Leadership exposure, availability, circulation and conversations throughout the business are genuinely meaningful, fun and educational without being condescending.

If the lessons preached by *The One Minute Manager* are applied consistently, the ease felt throughout the company hierarchy is palpable and the value that the organization gains from a team of players constantly looking for improvement can be priceless for performance improvements.

Through Blanchard's consulting organization, many large businesses have benefited from the application of Blanchard's principles. British Telecommunications deployed self-directed teams to provide customer service. Also in telecoms, Ericsson has used Blanchard's teachings to resolve leadership problems arising from rapid growth and merging cultures. In the banking sector, First Union has also used Blanchard for leadership training, which in turn has improved staff morale and retention.

Apparently, *The One Minute Manager* is now compulsory reading for some managers in American and Japanese industry.

How it dovetails with other guru theories

It's difficult to determine the impact Blanchard's small, priceless 'one minute' books has had on management styles. If a manager inculcates the right kind of behavior across the workplace, the impact this has on productivity, the working environment and individuals' feeling of enjoyment reaches far and wide; in fact, it is impossible to gauge.

Books such as *Who Moved My Cheese?* by Dr Spencer Johnson, are a clear example of the impact that Blanchard has had. Like *The One Minute Manager*, *Who Moved My Cheese?* also communicates its key messages through allegory, using a nest of mice. Through the mice's adventures, Johnson conveys the idea that success lies in proactive monitoring, swift adaptation to change and regular inspection of one's own premises – all key tenets of Blanchard's management theory, succinctly expressed in *The One Minute Manager*.

Validity today

No matter how much the corporate world changes, nothing will ever alter, or reduce, the validity of the message that our success in business leadership lies in how we engage and work with, and sometimes for, our employees.

Companies that really do appreciate and value their people are proven time and time again to be more profitable and more flexible than their less attentive competitors; hence they will have more resilient business models because of the care their teams administer, through constant engagement. Staff on whom we rely for profit creation can offer overwhelming, sometimes transformational thinking, and provide boundless sources of expertise and energy when motivated and encouraged.

The One Minute Manager may have been published in 1982, but the stories of learning through leadership it contains will be just as valid in a hundred years, perhaps even a thousand years, as they are now.

Astute business owners will always recognize the importance of harnessing brilliance in all people through the right kind of caring leadership; the approach Blanchard encapsulates in *The One Minute Manager*.

Ultimately, outstanding leadership with an engaged workforce will take a company from good to great, even with an average product. Blanchard didn't invent this concept, but he certainly presented it in the clearest and most compelling terms possible.

Edward de Bono

By Chris Fung

Name: Edward de Bono

Born: 1933

Expertise: Leading authority on creativity and the discipline and processes of thinking

Known for: De Bono has made several significant contributions to broadening the perception and definitions of thinking. Having invented the idea of lateral thinking and parallel thinking, he is a leading proponent of deliberate teaching of thinking in schools

Best-known titles: *The Use of Lateral Thinking* (1967); *Six Thinking Hats* (1985); *I Am Right, You Are Wrong* (1990); *Sur/Petition* (1992); *Teach Yourself How to Think* (1995); *How to Be More Interesting* (1998); *Simplicity* (1999)

Who is Edward de Bono?

Edward de Bono was born in Malta in 1933. He attended St Edward's College, Malta, during World War II and then the University of Malta, where he qualified in medicine. He went on to Christ Church, Oxford, as a Rhodes Scholar, where he gained an honors degree in psychology and physiology and then a DPhil in Medicine. He also holds a PhD from Cambridge and an MD from the University of Malta. He has held appointments at the universities of Oxford, London, Cambridge and Harvard.

What is de Bono known for?

Edward de Bono is known for introducing the concept of lateral thinking and the key contribution has been his understanding of the brain as a self-organizing system.

He is known as a leading authority in the field of creative thinking and the direct teaching of thinking as a key skill. He has been outspoken in his drive to teach thinking to people across all ages, cultures, belief systems and professional backgrounds, believing that these skills are not only vital to everyone but accessible and learnable to all, from pre-school children to multinational CEOs.

His methods have created groundbreaking ways of thinking about problems and have been able to help unleash latent creativity within individuals and organizations. The use of lateral thinking and his concepts of parallel thinking have provided a structured system of thinking serving not only large corporates, but individuals, politics and the education of children.

In 1985 he introduced his concept of the 'six thinking hats' as a way to evaluate and generate solutions to problems. This concept allowed an issue to be fully considered in a structured way, leading to constructive outcomes while reducing the impact of negative behaviors that are quite often found in group thinking. His idea of parallel thinking, whereby all participants, at any one moment in time, are looking and thinking in the same direction, combined with the structured process of the six thinking hats, has provided many companies, individuals and even governments with a practical set of tools to reach better decisions quicker.

The concepts

De Bono espouses the importance of thinking as a skill and believes Western thinking based around Socratic argument and debate is one-sided and does not take into account other important ways of thinking. Western thinking has been honed over many years to value judgment and critical thinking at the expense of an understanding of creative thinking, which is considered to be an Eastern approach.

The underlying concept and objective of six-hat thinking and parallel thinking is to provide a structured way of thinking through problems and issues that allows all aspects of a problem to be considered in a non-adversarial and constructive way.

How does six hats work?

In the six hats method, each hat represents a different direction of thinking. De Bono uses the example of four people looking at the different sides of a house. Each has a different view although they are all looking at the same thing.

The six hats system allows a group to see all views of a problem and come to an agreed solution. By systematically addressing the issues together as a group using this method, the outcomes are addressed in turn, objectively and with little ego and argument.

The result/outcomes

Once the system is used and practiced correctly, the result is that much better, more complicated decisions are reached more quickly. The result or agreed decision has consensus and buy-in from the whole group, as each participant is pulling in the same direction.

The emphasis is on 'what can be', not just 'what is'. In effect it is about designing a way forward – not about who is right or wrong.

The process

The six hats method is a thinking process – the ultimate human resource, according to de Bono. He states that the main difficulty of thinking is confusion, in that we try to do too much at once. Emotion, logic, hope, creativity, crowd and blur our focus. We effectively juggle too many balls at the same time and end up dropping them.

The six hats process allows a thinker to do one type of thinking at a time – the thinker separates logic from emotion from creativity from information.

The concept is that of six thinking hats (derived from putting on a thinking cap), with each hat a different color, representing a certain type of thinking.

The White Hat: Facts and Information	Examples applicable to business issues
White is neutral and objective: facts and figures Proven and checked facts: first class Facts believed to be true but not yet fully checked: second class facts Discipline of neutral thinking; data driven	Total sales from products introduced less than 12 months ago are £X p.a. Our growth rate is 15% p.a. over the past three years
Red Hat: Emotions and Feelings	**Examples applicable to business issues**
Red suggests anger, rage and emotions Emotional view This is how I feel about the matter Normal human emotions, likes, fear, dislike, suspicion Complex judgments: hunch, intuition, taste, sense, aesthetic	I'm very enthusiastic about the launch of the new product! I'm not convinced about the direction of the business strategy to move into international markets
Black Hat: Devil's Advocate and Caution	**Examples applicable to business issues**
Black is serious, careful and cautious. It points out the negatives, flaws and weaknesses in an idea Natural Western thinking/ logical: sensitized to find fault/ caution (devil's advocate) Risk assessment Can be used to identify weaknesses and threats	We will be facing strong competition if we enter that market We don't have the technical resources to manage such a large project without hiring new staff

Yellow Hat: Positives and Benefits	Examples applicable to business issues
Yellow is sunny and positive and constructive: covering hope and positive thinking Benefits that are logically based: scaled to proven, likely, not likely Can be used to define strengths and opportunities	We will be seen as the first to market and an innovator with this launch It will be challenging but we have an experienced team who will be able to deliver the results
Green Hat: New Ideas and Creativity	**Examples applicable to business issues**
Green is grass, fertile growth and indicates creativity and new ideas Search for alternatives Put forward possibilities/formal time to spend on creative thinking Lateral thinking (self-organizing, cuts across patterns of thinking) Use of provocation and movement	Why don't we ask our customers to design it in real time? Could we achieve the same result by using this alternative approach instead?
Blue Hat: Big Picture Process and Organization	**Examples applicable to business issues**
Blue is cool, sky and above all else. Blue is concerned with control, organization, a structured use of the other hats Chairman or facilitator role: permanent role/keeps the discipline	Let's talk through the objectives first and then we can delve into the detail OK, time to move on to some green hat thinking

Blue Hat: Big Picture Process and Organization	Examples applicable to business issues
Blue hat ends session by asking for outcome, summary/ conclusion, decision, solution or next steps	
Blue hat is outside the thinking on the subject – it is thinking of the process and the thinking that is required	
Helps manage focus and switch of focus to sensitize the brain	
Sets objectives, tasks: helps to set the direction	

In summary – a group is able to consider a problem collectively from a number of different angles and, in turn, negative or adversarial competition is reduced and ideas are given a platform to flourish. White hat facts, black hat dangers and green hat new ideas all form the basis of the thinking process.

Concept of argument vs parallel thinking

Western thinking and Socrates in essence believed argument was a chisel to unearth the hidden 'truth' under superficial appearances.

Parallel thinking is about constructive thinking and working from the basis that you need to look at different aspects of the situation. By systematically looking at all views, the subject is explored fully; opposing views are noted down in parallel. If a choice must be made later, then the attempt should be made; if not, the design must cover both possibilities.

The essence of parallel thinking is that at any one moment everyone involved is looking in the same direction. The direction can be changed as long as it is done together.

How real companies use de Bono's concepts

According to de Bono, in the 14 years from the book's first publication until its revised and updated edition in 1999 there have been a multitude of great examples of how large corporates, multinationals, governments, schools and international organizations used the six hats concept effectively.

A key benefit of the six hats system is not only in coming up with the actual solution to a multifaceted problem but in the actual speed with which a company or organization can achieve a decision.

De Bono describes examples of where ABB (a large Swedish corporation) used to spend 30 days on its project team discussions; however, through using the parallel thinking of the six hats method these discussions were reduced to two days. In another example, he tells of a senior IBM lab researcher reducing meeting times to a quarter of what they had been.

Statoil, a Norwegian oil company, had an oil rig problem that was costing $100,000 per day — until one of its certified six hats trainers introduced the method and the problem was solved in 12 minutes.

How it dovetails with other guru theories

The relatively well-known and frequently mentioned SWOT analysis credited to Albert Humphrey, who led a convention at Stanford University in the 1960s and 1970s using data from Fortune 500 companies, forms a neat subset of the six hats method of thinking. The SWOT analysis, which looks in turn at analyzing the strengths, weaknesses, opportunities and threats of a company, forms the basis for two of the six hats. The yellow hat effectively mirrors the strengths and opportunities of a problem while the black hat provides the forum for discussing the weaknesses and threats of the issue at hand.

Brainstorming as a structured method for creativity has helped many organizations become more creative. However, there have been limitations by the nature of the method itself. The six hats method has helped to improve and enhance the efficacy of brainstorming by addressing multiple angles of a problem and also, critically, to address the issue of human behavior in a group situation where people may not be comfortable being put on the spot to come up with ideas. By taking turns and allowing individuals their own thinking time, the six hats allow for more freedom to think.

Tony Buzan's 'mind maps' – which help bring out the best of creative thinking by allowing the mind to freely associate and think organically without the normal constraints of logical thinking bound by the physical attributes of rectangular pieces of paper and writing from left to right, top to bottom – is a great technique that can be combined with de Bono's six hats thinking method, to great effect. The combination of both methods can produce extremely effective results.

Validity today

The methods of Edward de Bono, from lateral thinking to using parallel thinking via the six hats method, are very valid today. De Bono himself believes them to be crucial to any development of thinking and argues that they should be a part of school curriculums.

As a method itself, six-hat thinking provides many benefits: it can be as simple as a structured way of thinking through any problem from all angles. This act of looking at a problem for a solution while considering all perspectives allows for more thorough analysis, buy-in and consensus, as well as removing the adversarial styles of thinking typical in Western thinking based on argument, along with ego-based decisions.

Most of our day-to-day thinking in a business context typically remains as black and white hat thinking, with quite often a lot of hidden red hat thinking that does not get aired in a constructive way. By allowing the full set of views in our thinking to be brought out in the open and the encouragement of more green and yellow hat thinking, the result of faster, better quality, consensus-seeking decisions can only be a positive thing!

Warren Buffett

By David Lester

Name: Warren Buffett

Born: 1930

Expertise: Legendary investor, currently worth $50bn, whose company has performed twice as well as the S&P 500 since 1965

Known for: A highly consistent and long-term approach to financial investments, which is known to many as the 'value investing' philosophy

Best-known titles: *The Snowball: Warren Buffett and the Business of Life,* Alice Schroeder (2009); *The Warren Buffett Way,* Miller, Hagstrom & Fisher (2005); *The Essays of Warren Buffett: Lessons for Corporate America,* L Cunningham *(1998)*

Who is Warren Buffett?

With nicknames such as 'the sage' and 'the oracle', Warren Buffett is renowned as one of the world's greatest investors, and millions of aspiring stock pickers know his proverbs off by heart. His company, Berkshire Hathaway, boasts a stock portfolio worth more than $52bn, encompassing multinationals such as Coca-Cola, MasterCard and Kraft Foods. Buffett himself is currently the third-richest man in the world (and America's second-richest), having held the top spot as recently as 2008.

What is Buffett known for?

Buffett is renowned for 'value investing', a particular, often unfashionable, approach to investing which had been initially developed by Benjamin Graham, author of *The Intelligent Investor* and father of the concept of value investing. Buffett invests primarily through the publicly quoted Berkshire Hathaway. Berkshire Hathaway was already an established, though small and little known, company when Buffett assumed control in 1965, and it has never given the world a brand-new product or service during his 46 years in charge.

Instead, Buffett has made his fortune through an innate genius for investment; for spotting a company which is undervalued by the stock market and which pays good, regular dividends; and holding each investment for many years, ignoring modern trends to buy and sell frequently. Since 1965, Berkshire has performed twice as well as the S&P 500; if you'd invested $10,000 in Berkshire back in the mid-1960s, your stake would be worth $49m today.

Unlike many multi-billionaires, Buffett lives a simple, self-effacing life. While others plough their fortunes into sprawling mansions and private helicopters, Buffett has lived in the same house since 1958, and enjoys plain, simple food rather than fancy fare – his favorite meal is reportedly a steak and French fries, washed down with a cherry coke.

Buffett made his first share purchase aged just 11 years and has changed millions of people's perceptions of investment forever. While he has never written complete books, he writes extensive reports about investing every year in Berkshire Hathaway's annual report, and these have become highly prized, influential documents – by far the best-read annual reports of any quoted company in the world.

The concepts

The roots of Buffett's incredible success can be traced back to his teenage years, soon after he made his first foray into the investment world, and to his studies at Columbia University. It was at Columbia that he was tutored by legendary investor Graham.

Graham turned the stock market on its head by eschewing chance and fads – as he perceived the more widespread practice of investing in 'growth-companies' – in favor of inexpensive, low-risk, often unloved investments. When investing, he focused on the 'intrinsic value' of a business rather than short-term vacillation in its share price, believing that the stock market regularly over-values companies and undervalues companies as emotional traders follow each other into or out of a particular share. By understanding what a company is really worth, it is then possible to buy its shares when the share price on the stock market is less than their true value, and sell them when it is above the true value.

Graham liked investors to regard themselves as part-owners of their investee businesses, rather than simple owners of a piece of paper (the share certificate) whose price fluctuated almost regardless of the intrinsic value of the company. His lessons remain integral to Buffett's approach to this day; in fact Buffett has described Graham as the second most influential person in his life, after his father.

One of the keys to Buffett's investing strategy is what he calls 'the float'. He likes buying companies which generate substantial cash flows, in particular insurance companies, which charge premiums often years before they need to pay out on any claims. This leads to large sums of cash which insurance companies invest – and which Buffett has been able to put to extremely good use. Insurance companies have long formed the backbone of Buffett's investment holdings.

Buffett's philosophy can be condensed into six key points, each illustrated by one of his famous quotes.

Rule No 1: Never lose money
Rule No 2: Never forget rule No 1

Many investors spend their lives hunting for hidden gems, turning over every stone in the search for the next market phenomenon, and homing in on chancy investments which have the potential for meteoric success – but also total failure. However, Buffett looks to minimize risk wherever possible, which he does by extensively researching potential companies to invest in, and by only buying when he believes the share price he buys at is less than the underlying value of those shares, based on reliable cash flow generation and the value of assets the company owns. This means he often invests in established, unglamorous companies.

Buffett is profoundly cynical of high-growth shares which are priced on the stock market at very high multiples of sales or profits; especially so when these companies have not ever made a profit. During the dotcom boom of 1999/2000, Buffett refused to buy into what he called the 'irrational exuberance' of online start-ups – preferring instead to stick to simple industries, such as energy and insurance. Ignoring the critics who mocked as his investments lagged behind the high-flying Nasdaq index during the dotcom boom, Buffett's investments thrived as the dotcom bubble burst, leaving more people impressed by his approach than ever. He remains cynical of tech companies to this day; another of his favorite maxims is 'never invest in something you don't understand'.

You can't buy into what is popular and do well

Buffett may be happy to back established names, but he generally finds them most attractive when they are forgotten or unloved. He has invested in both American Express and Geico when they were on the verge of insolvency, and bought substantial stakes in Goldman Sachs and GE in 2008 when their share prices were at almost historic lows. Buffett is a born opportunist, who is at his most effective during lean times. He urges investors to 'be fearful when others are greedy, and be greedy when others are fearful'.

Price is what you pay. Value is what you get

When Buffett is weighing up an investment, he looks beyond its immediate share price and explores the business fundamentals, and potential, of the company. He will closely examine a company's corporate structure, and its working practices, in an attempt to ascertain whether it has the foundations for sustainable success.

In terms of numbers, a business has to have a consistent trading history, low levels of debt, and a proven track record with reference to metrics such as return on equity, return on invested capital and profit margin. Buffett also looks for companies with 'the moat' – a barrier to other companies, often provided by a distinctive brand and a loyal customer base. Buffett is happy to pay a reasonable price for a company with pedigree; one of his many maxims is that 'it's far better to buy a wonderful company at a fair price than a fair company at a wonderful price'.

Our favorite holding period is forever

When Buffett does invest, he commits for the long term – in fact patience is arguably his definitive attribute as an investor. This attitude can be traced back to his first serious investment, when, after selling shares at $40, he had to watch helpless as they reached $200 in value – and to his apprenticeship under Benjamin Graham, who preached that investors should not be too concerned with short-term fluctuations in stock prices. Buffett is happy to wait years, even decades before selling stocks, rather than searching for a quick sale.

If a business does well, the stock eventually follows

Buffett looks upon each investment as a partnership – in his eyes, when an investor buys shares in a company, they should feel as though they are buying the company itself. Although now in his ninth decade, he remains as committed and as hands-on as ever. He proudly admits to reading hundreds upon hundreds of company reports every year, and immerses himself in all aspects of Berkshire's operation – often answering phone calls to his company personally. He demands daily reports on each of the many companies within Berkshire's aegis, and channels excess cash around his empire. Essentially, Berkshire operates as a private equity firm, not as a fund manager.

You can measure your success in life by how many of the people you want to love you actually do love you

For all Buffett's passion for investment, and unbridled work ethic, business isn't everything. A committed philanthropist, Buffett has pledged to give 99% of his fortune away to charitable causes, and, in tandem with long-time friend Bill Gates, has persuaded millions of other wealthy business leaders to make significant donations. In recent months Buffett has railed against the prevailing tax system – claiming super-rich individuals such as himself should actually pay more taxes.

How real companies use Buffett's concepts

It seems that every statement Buffett makes causes a ripple effect in the investment community; when, for example, he told reporters he paid close attention to the 'freight train index' which monitors the movement of raw materials around America, the index shot to the top of Google Trends almost instantly. Buffett has many prominent disciples in the investment community; a good example is Norman Rentrop, of global investment firm Rentrop Investment Office, who has based his success on Buffett's principles, particularly investing in undervalued public companies and pursuing private equity with a very long-term outlook.

It's impossible to quantify the impact of Buffett's concepts – no-one can know for sure how many companies and investors have taken inspiration from his words and career. However, it's safe to say that many millions of people have been exposed to Buffett's ideas. Buffett regularly writes opinion pieces for respected publications such as the *New York Times*, and books such as *The Snowball* have propagated his approach among a huge audience.

Buffett is also regarded as one of the investment world's most inspirational speakers, thanks to his earthy, homespun and humorous aphorisms. His speeches at Berkshire's annual shareholders' meeting attract more than 20,000 visitors every year – some have even dubbed the meeting 'the Woodstock of Capitalism', such is its enduring popularity.

In 2007, Buffett was named among *Time* magazine's 100 most influential people in the world, and he remains a seminal influence in the investment community today.

How it dovetails with other guru theories

Buffett's approach is to back great companies, and is compatible with many of the theories espoused by the gurus in this book. Perhaps the strongest links are with Michael Porter's 'competitive advantage', and with Jim Collins's focus on what makes great companies over time. Buffett seems in many ways to be at odds with modern digital thinkers such as Seth Godin or Chris

Anderson's 'long tail'. However, as Buffett has recently shown by investing in IBM, he is not opposed to buying technology companies where that is compatible with his own rules. But of course there will be many companies held up as shining examples by some digital-age thinkers which Buffett would not invest in; Amazon.com would seem a likely one, for example.

Validity today

Buffett's long-term, risk-averse approach seems more valid than ever in the current economic environment; his oft-cited criticism of derivatives back in the early years of the new millennium has only served to reinforce his reputation, as the concept of derivatives has pushed the financial world towards recession. Furthermore, Buffett has continued to make money during the downturn, burnishing his status as an investment genius.

There will continue to be outspoken investors who believe that Buffett's steady, straightforward approach is outdated. As the technology continues to develop, so more and more traditional businesses will be challenged. But Buffett began his investing days by buying into established companies often operating in declining markets, and did very well from it. His approach, carried out properly, would seem to remain as valid today as it was when he started.

Dale Carnegie

By Colin Barrow

Name: Dale Breckenridge Carnegie

Born: 1888; **died:** 1955

Expertise: Carnegie's core idea was to help people to see that it was perfectly possible to change other people's behavior by changing their own way of dealing with them, and in the process improve their own market value

---

Known for: Lecturing and training programs in self-confidence building, communication skills and leadership. His ideas survive as the curriculum at Dale Carnegie Training

---

Best-known titles: How to Win Friends and Influence People (1936); How to Stop Worrying and Start Living (1948); How To Enjoy Your Life and Your Job (1970)

Who is Dale Carnegie?

Carnegie's career started with a spell as a travelling salesman, followed by a brief acting career which in turn led him to giving classes in public speaking, teaching his students how to make persuasive presentations and build constructive relationships.

What is Carnegie known for?

In 1913 he formed the Dale Carnegie Institute and by 1931 had embarked on generating the material for his seminal work, *How to Win Friends and Influence People*. Whilst it's hard to claim any great intellectual originality for Carnegie's ideas, his claim to fame lies in the reach of his message. His book has been translated into more than 40 languages, selling more than 20 million copies. Dale Carnegie Training is delivered in every state in the US and in over 80 countries by some 2,700 instructors teaching in over 25 languages. Students range from Lee Iacocca, a former Chrysler chairman and Mary Kay Ashe, chairman of Mary Kay Cosmetics to salesmen, engineers and job hunters everywhere.

By 1912, aged just 24, Carnegie had stumbled into what was to become his lifetime's mission. He was running courses in public speaking for businesses and professionals in New York. At first, he concentrated on public speaking only, delivering courses 'designed to train adults, by actual experience, to think on their feet and express their ideas with more clarity, more effectiveness and more poise, both in business interviews and before groups'. Carnegie was also conducting courses for the American Institute of Electrical Engineers both in New York and Philadelphia. They came, he claimed, 'because they had finally realized, after years of observation and experience, that the highest-paid personnel in engineering are frequently not those who know the most about engineering, but the person who has technical knowledge plus the ability to express ideas, to assume leadership, and to arouse enthusiasm among people'.

Recognizing that most of his students needed training in 'the fine art of getting along with people in everyday business and social contact' every bit as much as polishing their public speaking skills, Carnegie prepared a short talk that he called 'How to Win Friends and Influence People'. It was short in the beginning, but it soon expanded to a 90-minute lecture.

One person who attended, Leon Shimkin, then a junior executive and later chairman at publishing house Simon & Schuster, was so impressed that he suggested Carnegie write a book based on his lectures. Carnegie wasn't at first interested but he agreed to let his secretary gather notes. He was eventually spurred on by the certainty that there was no competition. The University of Chicago and the United YMCA Schools had conducted a survey to find out what adults wanted to study. After health matters, the study revealed, their second interest was people; how to understand and get along with people; how to make people like you; and how to win others to your way of thinking. The committee responsible for the survey then searched exhaustively for a book to use as course material, but drew a blank. Two years later, between Shimkin, Carnegie and his secretary, *How to Win Friends and Influence People* was written and published.

The concepts

Carnegie didn't consider that he was developing theories. That word is only mentioned once in the introduction to his book.

Method, in contrast, is a word liberally sprayed around every chapter. He recommended that you should read his work 'with a crayon, pencil, pen, magic marker, or highlighter in your hand. When you come across a suggestion that you feel you can use, draw a line beside it'.

His book is divided into four parts headed: 'Fundamental Techniques in Handling People'; 'How to Win People to Your Way of Thinking'; 'Six Ways to Make People Like You'; and 'Be a Leader'. Each part has a number of chapters from which Carnegie drew pithy, single-sentence messages that he called 'principles' (see the figure on p.63).

His style throughout is to introduce an idea, usually through reference to accepted research findings, followed by an illustration of how that idea has been applied in everyday affairs. For example, his first principle, 'Don't criticize, condemn or complain', starts with a reference to BF Skinner, Edgar Pierce professor of psychology at Harvard University. Carnegie states, 'the world-famous psychologist, proved through his experiments that an animal rewarded for good behavior will learn much more rapidly and retain what it learns far more effectively than an animal punished for bad behavior. Later studies have shown that the same applies to humans. By criticizing, we do not make lasting changes and often incur resentment.'

Carnegie then goes on to tell the story of one George B Johnston of Enid, Oklahoma, the safety coordinator for an engineering company, one of whose responsibilities was to see that employees wear their hard hats whenever they are on the job in the field. At first, whenever he came across workers who were not wearing hard hats, he would remind them of the regulation and that they must comply. The result was usually a sullen acceptance, with hats being removed as soon as he was out of sight. Carnegie then describes what happened when Johnston tried a different approach. 'The next time he found some of the workers not wearing their hard hat, he asked if the hats were uncomfortable or did not fit properly. Then he reminded the men in a pleasant tone of voice that the hat was designed to protect them from injury and suggested that it always be worn on the job. The result was increased compliance with the regulation with no resentment or emotional upset'.

In Part 2: 'Six Ways to Make People Like You', Carnegie blends ancient history, quoting Roman poet Publilius Syrus's remark, 'We are interested in others when they are interested in us', with observations of what he saw as self-evident truths. Challenging his reader to 'study the technique of the greatest winner of friends the world has ever known', he puts forward the dog as 'the only animal that doesn't have to work for a living? A hen has to lay eggs, a cow has to give milk, and a canary has to sing. But a dog makes his living by giving you nothing but love.'

Carnegie didn't claim to always be able to apply all his principles all of the time. 'For example', he said, 'when you are displeased, it is much easier to criticize and condemn than it is to try to understand the other person's viewpoint. It is frequently easier to find fault than to find praise. It is more natural to talk about what you want than to talk about what the other person wants and so on. So, as you read this book, remember that you are not merely trying to acquire information. You are attempting to form new habits. Ah yes, you are attempting a new way of life. That will require time and persistence and daily application.'

How real companies use Carnegie's concepts

Perhaps the most powerful endorsement of Carnegie's methods is the ringing praise Warren Buffett, the world's third-richest man, gives it. 'The most important degree that I have', is how Buffett described his experience of attending a Dale Carnegie Training course in January 1952. Buffett's biographer, Alice Schroeder, documented 13 other references to Carnegie and the influence Buffett attributes to the lessons from *How to Win Friends and Influence People*. Buffett first came across the book on his grandfather's bookshelf when he was 'eight or nine'. Buffett follows Carnegie's principles in his business methods, but he doesn't just accept them blindly. Schroeder reveals that he conducted a statistical analysis of what happened if he did follow Dale Carnegie's principles and what happened if he didn't. The numbers proved that the rules worked.

Buffett is just one of millions who have been influenced by Carnegie's work. Jonathan Yardley, book critic at *The Washington Post* and the 1981 recipient of the Pulitzer Prize for Criticism, when asked for the '10 books that shaped the American character', ranked Carnegie alongside Thoreau, Whitman, Twain and Hemingway.

Carnegie was nothing if not rigorous in checking out everyone with anything to contribute to his subject. In preparation, he states in the introduction, 'I read everything that I could find on the subject – everything from newspaper columns, magazine articles, records of the family courts, the writings of the old philosophers and the new psychologists'. He hired a researcher who spent 18 months trawling libraries, reading through 'erudite tomes on psychology, poring over hundreds of magazine articles, searching through countless biographies, trying to ascertain how the great leaders of all ages had dealt with people'. Carnegie interviewed scores of successful people, including Marconi, Edison and Franklin D Roosevelt. He spoke with film stars, including Clark Gable and Mary Pickford, trying to discover the techniques they used in human relations.

How it dovetails with other guru theories

Carnegie's ideas fit well with contemporary research studies such as those carried out by Harvard Business School professor Elton Mayo's renowned Hawthorne Studies. His research was conducted between 1927 and 1932 at the Western Electric Hawthorne Works in Chicago. Starting out to see what effect illumination had on productivity, Mayo moved on to see how fatigue and monotony fitted into the equation by varying rest breaks, temperature, humidity and work hours, even providing a free meal at one point. Working with a team of six women, Mayo changed every parameter he could think of, including increasing and decreasing working hours and rest breaks; finally he returned to the original conditions. Every change resulted in an improvement in productivity, except when two 10-minute pauses morning and afternoon were expanded to six five-minute pauses. These frequent work pauses, they felt, upset their work rhythm. Mayo's conclusion was that showing 'someone upstairs cares', and engendering a sense of ownership and responsibility, were important motivators that could be harnessed by management.

After Mayo came a flurry of theories on motivation. William McDougall, in his book *The Energies of Men* (1932, Methuen), listed 18 basic needs that he referred to as instincts (e.g. curiosity, self-assertion, submission). HA Murray, assistant director of the Harvard Psychological Clinic, catalogued 20 core psychological needs, including achievement, affiliation and power. Although never directly acknowledged, Carnegie's work seems to have influenced the thinking of subsequent academic thinkers. Abraham Maslow, who taught at Brandeis University, Boston, developed and popularized a hierarchy of needs (1943) showing some parallels with Carnegie's list of eight things that most people want (see figure opposite). Frederick Herzberg, professor of psychology at Case Western Reserve University in Cleveland, US, listed 'recognition: everyone likes their hard work to be acknowledged' as one of five key workplace motivators. Carnegie's principle, 'Praise the slightest improvement and praise every improvement. Be hearty in your approbation and lavish in your praise', makes much the same observation.

Validity today

Carnegie's ideas are as relevant today as when he first set them down in writing. His widow, Dorothy, oversaw a revised edition of How to Win Friends and Influence People in 1981, updating some of the language and examples 'to clarify and strengthen the book for a modern reader without tampering with the content'. In October 2011 a second revision was published, How to Win Friends, and Influence People in the Digital Age which re-imagined the original book for the digital age and updated and reframed Carnegie's insights about communication, self-expression and leadership to accommodate social networking sites and email. An iPhone app version of the original book, complete with video clips, charts, tips and a 'daily dose of confidence' came out in 2010 and was the top-selling paid business app in the iTunes store. A version for BlackBerry followed.

Carnegie and Maslow compared

Carnegie

Some of the things most people want include:

1. Health and the preservation of life.
2. Food.
3. Sleep.
4. Money and the things money will buy.
5. Life in the hereafter.
6. Sexual gratification.
7. The well-being of our children.
8. A feeling of importance.

Maslow's hierarchy of needs

Self-actualisation
Personal growth and fulfilment

Esteem
Achievement, status and reputation

Social
The need for friends and associations

Safety
The need to feel safe, secure and protected

Physiological
The most basic needs – air, water, food and sleep

FUNDAMENTAL TECHNIQUES IN HANDLING PEOPLE
Don't criticize, condemn or complain.
Give honest and sincere appreciation.
Arouse in the other person an eager want.

BE A LEADER
Begin with praise and honest appreciation.
Call attention to people's mistakes indirectly.
Talk about your own mistakes before criticizing the other person.
Ask questions instead of giving direct orders.
Let the other person save face.
Praise the slightest improvement and praise every improvement. Be 'hearty in your approbation and lavish in your praise.'
Give the other person a fine reputation to live up to.
Use encouragement. Make the fault seem easy to correct.
Make the other person happy about doing the thing you suggest.

HOW TO WIN PEOPLE TO YOUR WAY OF THINKING
The only way to get the best of an argument is to avoid it.
Show respect for the other person's opinions. Never say, 'You're wrong.'
If you are wrong, admit it quickly and emphatically.
Begin in a friendly way.
Get the other person saying 'yes, yes' immediately.
Let the other person do a great deal of the talking.
Let the other person feel that the idea is his or hers.
Try honestly to see things from the other person's point of view.
Be sympathetic with the other person's ideas and desires.
Appeal to the nobler motives.
Dramatize your ideas.
Throw down a challenge.

SIX WAYS TO MAKE PEOPLE LIKE YOU
Become genuinely interested in other people.
Smile.

Robert Cialdini

By Clive Rich

Name: Robert B Cialdini

Born: 1945

Expertise: Persuasion and influencing in business

Known for: Books on the science of influencing, and identifying the six 'weapons of influence'

Best-known publications: *Influence: The Psychology of Persuasion* (1984); *Influence: Science and Practice* (5th edition 2009); *Yes!: 50 Scientifically Proven Ways to be Persuasive* (2008), with NJ Goldstein and SJ Martin

Who is Robert Cialdini?

Robert Cialdini has spent his entire career researching the science of influencing. *Influence* has sold over two million copies worldwide and *Fortune Magazine* lists it in its 75 smartest business books. He is currently Regents professor emeritus of psychology and marketing at Arizona State University.

What is Cialdini known for?

Robert Cialdini is an experimental social psychologist specializing in how people are influenced. His interest stems from a self-confessed life as a 'patsy'. As he puts it, 'For as long as I can recall, I've been an easy mark for the pitches of peddlers, fund raisers and operators ... with personally disquieting frequency.'

This accounts for his research into the 'psychology of compliance'. Partly he has carried out experiments in the lab and on college students, but he quickly realized that he needed to go out in the field and work with what he terms 'compliance professionals' – those whose job it is to persuade us to part with our money. So, for nearly three years he worked with sales operators, fund raisers, recruiters and others to find out the secrets of their success as influencers. This practical research formed the basis of *Influence: The Psychology of Persuasion*.

The concepts

Cialdini has identified six principles of influence which are favored by such compliance professionals and his book identifies and explains each of these principles in turn.

The starting point is to realize that we all have patterns of automated behavior which cause us to respond in predictable ways to specific stimuli. Just as a chicken will respond automatically and maternally to the 'cheep cheep' noise of its chicks, we have certain conditioned responses that help us navigate the world successfully. These responses mean that we don't have to catalogue, appraise and calibrate every decision we make.

However, these automated responses make us vulnerable to operators who stimulate those responses to their own advantage. For example, a typical example of a conditioned response would be 'if it's expensive it must be good'. This is rooted in conditioning we receive from childhood which says 'you get what you pay for'. Equally we are programed to respond to contrast. If two different things are presented to us one after the other we exaggerate the difference between them. Exploiters can also take advantage of this automated response to influence us.

Having established that the aim of influencers is always to elicit one of these auto-responses, Cialdini goes on to explain what the six principles of influence are.

1. The principle of 'reciprocity'

This rule tells us that we have to repay in kind what another person has provided us. If someone buys us a birthday gift, we feel obligated to buy one for them too. The principle of reciprocity operates even where we don't particularly like the person who initiates the exchange. The principle is particularly effective when what we are responding to is a 'concession' made by someone else. So skilled influencers might propose a large price first, and then retreat to a more reasonable proposal. The act of making a concession is likely to induce in the customer a sense of obligation to make a concession in return by buying something.

2. The principle of 'consistency to commitment'

When we have made a small commitment to a particular course of action we have an in-built desire to remain consistent to that course of action so as to justify our earlier decision. In addition, if we have made a commitment publicly, we are particularly inclined to stick with it so as to avoid losing face.

Exploiters wanting to influence us understand this principle, knowing that if we will allow them this small commitment then a bigger one will follow. For example, perhaps retailers will ask us to enter into a written competition to endorse a particular product. They know that once we have done that we will want to stick with that 'commitment' and go on to buy it. Particularly insidious influencers will get us to make a commitment to a low price, and then withdraw the price and say they made a mistake. Once we are committed we will be unlikely to change our mind.

3. The principle of 'social proof'

We determine whether something is correct by identifying what other people think is correct. This is especially true in ambiguous situations – for example where groups of people witness what may be a crime or an accident. Generally, unless one person moves to help the victim then nobody will, as everybody assumes that the kind of unflustered indifference exhibited by the other bystanders is 'the norm'. If, however, anyone makes that commitment to get involved, then lots of other people feel it's okay to get involved too. We all look for this vindication, and often its application makes sense in our daily lives; if other people are doing something it may well be the right thing to do. However, this automated response can lead us astray – a news item on suicides often seems to provoke a rash of copycat suicides.

4. The principle of 'liking'

We tend to be influenced more by people we like than by those that we don't. Sadly, in making 'liking' decisions we often rely on shallow factors. We like people who are good looking rather than those who are ugly. We like people who are more 'like us', because they share our interests and passions. We like people who compliment and flatter us. We like people with whom we share cooperative exercises – think why companies send employees on outward bound trips where they have to bond over team exercises where cooperation is required. Moreover, we like things that are 'associated' with people we like – we assume that the products and services they are associated with must have the same positive attributes that we assign to them, and we want to link ourselves with that good association, as that also makes us feel better about ourselves.

This is fertile ground for those who seek to influence us – especially compliance professionals who may be seeking to exercise an unfair advantage, by trying to make sure we like them.

5. The 'authority' principle

There is a deep-seated sense of duty to authority in all of us. Authority figures loom large in our life from an early age – parents, teachers, religious figures – and it seems that their influence persists into later life.

It is for this reason that con artists frequently like to pose as authority figures – e.g. doctors, judges or professors, or 'titled' individuals. Uniforms also convey a sense of authority – even a civilian 'uniform' such as a well-cut suit.

Influencers can subvert this principle by vesting their offering with some kind of 'authority' (whether bogus or otherwise) in order to incline us to buy it.

6. The 'scarcity' principle

The idea of potential loss plays a large role in human decision making. In fact people seem to be more motivated by the thought of losing something than by the thought of gaining something of equal value. Scarcity works as a motivator partly because we hate to lose freedoms (such as a freedom of choice) that we already have. So scarcity works especially well when something that was previously available in abundance becomes scarce.

'Deadline' tactics are a good example of the scarcity tactic at work – people often find themselves doing what they wouldn't normally do, on the basis that the time to do so is shrinking. The real or pretended introduction of another potential buyer also evokes the scarcity principle.

How real companies use Cialdini's concepts

Cialdini gives numerous examples of how companies use each of these principles in turn.

Automated behavior

Cialdini gives the example of a jeweler who has found that the best way to shift hard-to-sell items is to substantially *increase* their price! This activates the automated response that 'if it's expensive it must be good'.

Equally, Cialdini describes how clothes retailers are often trained to sell someone an expensive suit first, and then try to sell them the accessories afterwards. The reason for this is that having spent a lot on a suit, the price of the accessories doesn't seem so great by contrast, and so we are more likely to buy.

The principle of reciprocity

Cialdini describes how successful the Krishna movement was in raising funds after it adopted a policy of giving people a free flower at airports and then asking for money. Many companies are so keen to provide us with free 'samples' – these samples create an unconscious sense of obligation which makes it more likely that we will buy something in return.

The principle of consistency to commitment

Toy manufacturers will seek to build up sales for January and February (traditionally poor months for toy sales) by driving customers to stores in December, having deliberately created shortages of big-name toys. They know that, having made the original commitment to buy that toy but failed, the punters will turn up again in January and February to attempt to purchase.

The principle of social proof

Advertisers refer to testimonials from members of the public to support their campaigns – 'in tests eight out of 10 owners said their dog preferred "x" dog-food'. Advertisers sometimes film 'man in the street' endorsements for their products when either the participant is an actor or doesn't know he is being filmed. The aim is to create an impression of social proof from our peers so that we will be more influenced to buy.

The principle of liking

Companies and retailers know that men are more likely to buy from sales reps who are pretty women – men assume the car is as likable as the model. All of us are influenced by sales reps who take the time to find out about our background and interests and then present their own background so as to seem more like us. It may emerge that, spookily, they have the same interest in sport, and know very well the area of the country we come from, and that predisposes us towards the product they are selling. They may choose to seem like us in other ways too – for example by mirroring our language, mood or body posture.

The authority principle

Cialdini shows how compliance professionals use this tactic ruthlessly – for example using authority figures in their advertising in order to encourage us to buy something. He refers to the use of Robert Young (an actor who played a doctor in a TV series) to lend authority to the commercials for Sanka coffee.

The scarcity principle

Manufacturers will produce 'limited editions'. Or sales reps will tell us that they only have 'one more item left in the stock room'. Or they may tell us that they are actually out of stock, but then miraculously source an item if we commit to buying it prior to its revelation. This is a particularly clever application of the principle, because the customer is asked to make a commitment when the product looks least available and is therefore most desirable.

How it dovetails with other guru theories

Cialdini has influenced other thinkers on the subject – consciously or otherwise. For example, Gladwell's *Tipping Point* owes something to the principle of social proof described by Cialdini. Equally his claim in *Blink* that our instinctive reaction is often the right one chimes with Cialdini's principle that we often operate on the basis of automated cues. Trigger these cues and you get the 'click/whirr' automatic response described by Cialdini which can be used as a tool of influence. The link with James Surowiecki's *Wisdom of Crowds* seems fairly direct, since Cialdini's principle of social proof underlies the crowd-based decisions. There is also a link with modern guru works such as *Nudge: Improving Decisions about Health* by Thaler and Sunstein. *Nudge* argues that nudging people with small incentives is a great way to influence them. Small incentives build small commitments, and Cialdini argues that influencing small commitments leads to greater commitments.

Validity today

Cialdini's principles still seem relevant and he is still very active teaching and lecturing on the science of influence. For example, 'nudge' theory as espoused by Thaler and Sunstein has been a very hot topic in political circles for the last couple of years. The theory argues that instead of ordering people around you can get them to do the right thing by finding out why they choose and then giving them small incentives so that they choose well. This sounds like classic Cialdini terrain. President Obama was very focused on this theory in his election campaign and used a secret 'consortium of behavioral scientists' to put 'nudge' theory into practice. Thaler and Sunstein have since become influential at the White House. In 2008 Thaler met David Cameron, and now No. 10 has its own 'behavioral insight' or 'nudge' team. That same year Cameron put 'nudge' on a summer reading list for Tory MPs. What else was on the list? Robert Cialdini's *The Psychology of Persuasion*, for one.

Jim Collins

By Dominic Monkhouse

Name: James C 'Jim' Collins, III

Born: 1958

Expertise: The common characteristics that drive company growth

Known for: Defining the underlying variables that enable any type of organization to make the leap from good to great while others only remain 'good'

Best-known titles: *Built to Last: Successful Habits of Visionary Companies* (1994); *Good to Great: Why Some Companies Make the Leap ... And Others Don't* (2001); *How the Mighty Fall: And Why Some Companies Never Give In* (2009)

Who is Jim Collins?

Jim Collins is a highly regarded business consultant, researcher, author and lecturer on what makes companies achieve growth, become great and stay exceptional. The influence of Collins' work has been recognized by *Fortune*, *The Wall Street Journal*, *New York Times*, *Business Week*, *Harvard Business Review* and *Fast Company*.

What is Collins known for?

Collins' first book, *Built to Last: Successful Habits of Visionary Companies*, was a fixture on the *Business Week* bestseller list for more than six years. It analyzes why some companies are able to achieve and sustain success through multiple generations of business leaders. By identifying the common characteristics of highly visionary companies, Collins and co-author Jerry Porras provide the visionary insight to influence management on how to stay ahead of competitors.

Collins' second book, *Good to Great: Why Some Companies Make the Leap ... And Others Don't*, has sold over three million copies. The book addresses a single question – can good companies become great, and if so how? Based on five years of painstaking research, Collins identifies the key concepts that enable companies to become great and, in the process, achieve stock market returns an average of six times greater than market performance over a 15-year period.

Collins' third book, *How the Mighty Fall: And Why Some Companies Never Give In*, presents the hope that leaders can fend off and reverse declining fortunes. The book reveals that the fate of companies is largely self-inflicted, rather than determined by circumstances or history.

The concepts

The key message of *Good to Great*, in Collins' words, is that 'greatness is not a matter of circumstance; greatness is largely a matter of conscious choice and discipline'. Good is the enemy of great. By settling for a B grade performance, rather than an A+, an organization is setting a course for mediocrity at best and, more often, the scrap heap.

Collins challenges business leaders to forget the rules they have learned in trying to be a 'good business' and not waste their time aiming for the 'miracle moment' when everything suddenly just falls into place and the business really takes off.

The flywheel effect

Collins uses the 'flywheel effect' as an analogy to explain how the change from good to great happens. The flywheel represents the business, and executives concentrate on how to make it move and create momentum in order to generate profits. Getting the flywheel to move takes effort. You keep pushing and it moves a little faster, and by pushing steadily, it moves faster still. By maintaining this focus, eventually the business reaches a breakthrough when the flywheel spins and accelerates of its own accord, without the need to keep pushing it so hard. Collins reveals the flywheel effect is what it feels like when you're inside a company that crosses the divide from good to great.

Collins and his research team describe how the formula for turning good into great is not revolution; instead, the secret is a down-to-earth, continuously pragmatic approach. It's a process of build-up that results in breakthrough. Collins presents a roadmap for businesses based on three key stages: disciplined people, disciplined thought and disciplined action. Each of these stages involves two key concepts that offer practical lessons and advice.

Disciplined people

Collins' research found a common empirical truth: for every company that became great, it had 'level 5 leadership' at the helm at the time of transition. A 'level 5 leader' is able to channel their ego needs away from themselves and into the larger goal of building a great company. In personality terms, these leaders are often reserved, humble, courteous and simultaneously, ruthless, focused and highly ambitious – for the company rather than themselves. Critically, they inspire employees with their own standards rather than flashy strategies or initiatives. Level 5 sits at the pinnacle of a hierarchy of executive capabilities, and while Collins recognizes gaining each of these skill levels doesn't have to be a straight-line progression, all level 5 leaders display all five of these key leadership characteristics.

Good-to-great leaders might be expected to begin by setting a new vision and strategy. In fact, what these leaders do first is to get the right people 'on the bus'. Of course, give people a chance, but act to deselect staff that cannot embody the culture of greatness and work to get the right people into the right seats. Having a people vision and making big investments in rigorous hiring of the right staff becomes a virtuous circle.

With the right people in place, there is no need to worry about motivating them. The right people are self-motivated. The consequence of heading for a destination without sorting out first who will help you get there is that when direction needs to change, the team may not be willing to take the journey. And, even if the journey does following its intended path, Collins asserts that if you have the wrong people, you still won't achieve greatness. Great vision with mediocre people still produces mediocre results.

Disciplined thought

Collins urges leaders to 'confront the brutal facts (yet never lose faith)'. However bad it gets, great leaders don't hide from the brutal truth: instead they show faith in the future. If you can't keep up with competitors, you need to change course. If your cost base is too high, you need to make redundancies. Whatever the situation, the willingness of the company to assess, listen and take action in the face of adversity is part of being great. Collins advocates a culture of openness and honesty, where responsibility for success lies collectively within the team, but ultimately, responsibility for failure sits with the business leader. That business leader must have the discipline to meet challenges head on.

Great leaders have unwavering faith that they will prevail in the end, no matter what the brutal facts of the current reality. Hope and teamwork are vital components of greatness and inspirational leaders that stand up to be counted when the going gets tough are indispensable.

The 'hedgehog' concept

All great leaders, according to Collins are 'hedgehogs'. Under this 'hedgehog concept', they know one big thing, rather than lots of smaller things and are able to crystallize a complex world into a single, organizing, galvanizing idea. This is not to say that great leaders are simplistic themselves, rather that they have the power of thought to develop penetrating insight and deep understanding of the path to take.

Finding the 'hedgehog concept' for an organization comes about on alignment of three intersecting circles that ask the following questions.

- What can we be best at in the world?
- What drives the economy of our business?
- What are our core people deeply passionate about?

The sentiment here is don't try to do 10 things well; find the one thing you can do better than anyone else and stick to it.

Disciplined action

Just say no. Not all growth is good, and having the discipline to say no to opportunities outside of your core focus is part of the discipline required throughout the company to get on the path to greatness. Collins advocates that business leaders should not only have a 'to do' list, but a 'stop doing' list as well. Good-to-great leaders distinguish themselves by their iron discipline to stop doing anything and everything that doesn't fit within their hedgehog concept.

A culture of discipline is a by-product of disciplined people conducting disciplined thought. Collectively these people create a culture where hierarchy is not required and bureaucracy is impossible. This culture of discipline, hand in hand with an ethic of entrepreneurship, creates the magic combination of unlocking great performance.

Good-to-great companies think differently about technology. They never use it to trigger a transformation, but put it to good use to accelerate the flywheel effect. Collins asserts that the technology by itself is never a primary root cause of either greatness or decline.

How real companies use Collins' concepts

Kimberley Clark, the world's leading paper-based consumer products company, is one of Collins' own examples of a company that became great — in this case by accepting the brutal truth and finding its hedgehog concept. From 1971, 'the stodgy old paper company' whose stock had fallen 36% behind the market in the previous decade undertook a remarkable transformation. Darwin Smith, then CEO, made a gutsy decision to 'sell the mills'; in effect to stop doing what Kimberly Clark had been doing since it began. Smith took a 'succeed or die' position, taking on Procter & Gamble to enter the consumer products market with brands such as Kleenex and Huggies. For 20 years, he stuck to his belief, ending up beating P&G in three-quarters of its competing lines and multiplying the company's market capitalization by over four times.

How it dovetails with other guru theories

Collins described *Good to Great* as the prequel to *Built to Last*. In *Built to Last*, Collins systematically distinguishes the great from the average. A set of core values is the solution for ongoing greatness, which led him to consider how these companies became great in the first place.

Collins' work on the 'hedgehog concept' shows similarities with the *Blue Ocean Strategy* (2005) by W Chan Kim and Renée Mauborgne, where the first of four key strategies is to create uncontested market space. Defining the business's singularity is aligned to the single focus of the hedgehog.

Guy Kawasaki, author of several books, including *Rules for Revolutionaries*, sums up the 'first who' principle when he writes, 'A players hire A+ players – B players hire C players.' Like Collins, Kawasaki believes that great people hire great people. On the other hand, mediocre people hire candidates who are not as good as they are. The slippery slope of hiring Z players, or Kawasaki's 'bozo effect', shows similar thinking in terms of the ability to recruit quality people as the crucial first step to building a successful organization.

Validity today

The *Good to Great* concepts are very much still of value, but the underlying research from which Collins drew his theories has been criticized. The study only focuses on US companies. American culture loves the myth of the 'lone hero', glorifying the CEOs responsible for these corporate feats of greatness. However, in other parts of the world, successful culture is determined by groups of people, not individuals. All organizations benefit from great leadership, but ultimately it takes a team effort to achieve something great.

There is also a gap in the scope of Collins' research. Of the 1,435 companies studied, none is from the high-tech industry. These businesses often have a far shorter history and follow a very different growth trajectory. Intel, in many people's eyes, has always been great.

The flywheel effect still holds, but in today's business world the wheel is turning faster. The global social networking phenomenon, Facebook, is a prime example of accelerated greatness. Despite being only five years old, it has generated incredible share performance. Collins' view that a company requires time and consistently disciplined effort over several years needs a refresh. Greatness doesn't have to come with age.

Stephen Covey

By Colin Barrow

Name: Stephen R Covey

Born: 1932

Expertise: Internationally respected expert on leadership techniques and personal effectiveness. Currently a professor at the Jon M Hunstman School of Business at Utah State University

Known for: Adaptation of religious life principles into management principles to encourage a self-disciplined approach for managers

Best-known titles: *The 7 Habits of Highly Effective People* (1989); *Spiritual Roots of Human Relations* (1970); *The Divine Center* (1982); *Principle Centered Leadership* (1992); *First Things First*, co-authored with Roger and Rebecca Merrill (1994); *Living the Seven Habits* (2000); *The 8th Habit: From Effectiveness to Greatness* (2004); *The Leader in Me – How Schools and Parents Around the World are Inspiring Greatness, One Child at a Time* (2008)

Who is Stephen Covey?

Covey took BS in Business administration at the University of Utah, has a Harvard MBA and a doctorate in Religious Education (DRE) from the Brigham Young University, where he worked as a professor of business management and organizational behavior. His *7 Habits* book has sold over 20 million copies and been translated into 38 languages.

What is Covey known for?

Covey, a practicing member of The Church of Jesus Christ of Latter-day Saints (Mormons), started on his seminal work when, as an MBA student at Harvard, he preached occasionally on Boston Common. Later whilst holding teaching missions for his church Covey prepared the ground for *The Divine Center*. In this he essentially communicates Mormon truths to non-Mormons by simply changing his vocabulary to more familiar ideas and concepts. This book was almost a dummy run for *7 Habits* that followed seven years later. Rather than showing the principle of 'centering one's life on Christ' and examining the 12 'centers' such as 'security', 'guidance', 'wisdom', and 'power', *7 Habits* takes a secular look at how we can improve.

His ideas have seen him listed by *Time* magazine as one of its 25 most influential Americans and this book was chosen as the most influential business book of the 20th century by *Forbes* magazine. In 2010 he was appointed a tenured professor of the Jon M Huntsman School of Business at Utah State University to lead the teaching in 'principle-centered leadership'.

The concepts

The book is prefaced with these words of Aristotle, 'We are what we repeatedly do. Excellence, then, is not an act, but a habit.' Covey's key concept is that by changing certain habits, though it is usually a slow and often painful process, we can become more effective. Acquiring the seven habits of effectiveness that Covey describes takes us through the stages of character development. Habits 1 through 3 make up the 'private victory': where we go from dependence to independence by taking responsibility for our own lives. Acquiring habits 4 through 6 is our 'public victory'. Once independent, we learn to be interdependent, to succeed with other people. The seventh habit makes all the others possible – periodically renewing ourselves in mind, body and spirit.

Covey's 7 habits

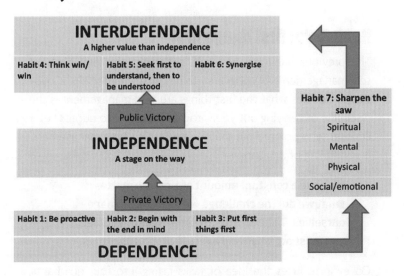

Habit 1: Be proactive

This is concerned with exploring ways to take control of events rather than being the victim of circumstance. Covey suggests testing if you have the proactive habit by noting how often you use these expressions.

'That's the way I am' = There's nothing I can do about it.
'He makes me so mad!' = My emotional life is outside my control.
'I have to do it' = I'm not free to choose my own actions.

Habit 2: Begin with the end in mind

Here Covey recommends developing a personal mission statement and acquiring what he calls the habit of personal leadership so that you can keep steering in the right direction despite changing circumstances. Developing this habit allows you to concentrate most of your energies on activities relevant to your end goal, avoiding distractions and in the process becoming more productive and successful.

Habit 3: Put first things first

The previous habit involves self-leadership; this one is about self-management: putting first things first. Leadership, Covey states, 'decides what the first things are, and management is the discipline of carrying out your program'. Covey also quotes Peter Drucker, who pointed out that the expression 'time management' is something of a misnomer:

> We have a constant amount of time, no matter what we do; the challenge we face is to manage ourselves. To be an effective manager of yourself, you must organize and execute around priorities.

Covey introduces the idea of tasks fitting into four quadrants, with 'important – not important' on one continuum and 'urgent – not urgent' on the other.

Covey's 4-quadrant time manager

Quadrant I Urgent Important	Quadrant II Not Urgent Important
Crises	Building relationships
Some meetings	Planning strategy
Pressing problems	Building the team
Dealing with deadlines	Developing staff
	Delegating tasks

Quadrant III Urgent Not Important	Quadrant IV Not Urgent Not Important
Interruptions	Trivia
Some mail, reports	Time wasters
Some meetings	Some mail
Pressing matters	Personal issues not related to job
Popular activities	

Reports, meetings, calls, interruptions and the occasional genuine crisis will drag us into spending time in quadrants I and III. Time spent on quadrant IV activities is only for those determined to fail. (Don't confuse quadrant IV with any of the activities recommended in habit, these are all definitely quadrant II tasks that need to be timetabled into your life.)

Covey recommends a way to up your time on quadrant II tasks. Write down two or three important results you feel you should accomplish during the next seven days. At least some of these goals should be quadrant II activities.

Look at the week ahead with your goals in mind and block out the time each day to achieve them. With your key goals locked in, see what time is left for everything else! How well you succeed depends on how resilient and determined you are in defending your most important priorities.

Habit 4: Think win/win

Covey's complete description is 'win/win – or no deal'. This is one of what he calls the 'paradigms of human interaction'. The others – win/lose, lose/win, lose/lose are to be avoided. He recommends that your attitude should be, 'I want to win, and I want you to win. If we can't hammer something out under those conditions, let's agree that we won't make a deal this time. Maybe we'll make one in the future.' Win/win is based on the assumption that there is plenty for everyone, and that success follows a cooperative approach more naturally than the confrontation of win-or-lose; in short, a sophisticated twist on the glass half full or half empty attitude to life.

Habit 5: Seek first to understand and then to be understood

The key word in mastering this habit is 'listen'. Listen to your colleagues, family, friends, customers – but not, as Covey states, 'with intent to reply, to convince, to manipulate. Listen simply to understand, to see how the other party sees things.' The skill he advocates here is empathy. Covey explains 'empathy is not sympathy. Sympathy is a form of agreement, a judgment. The essence of empathic listening is not that you agree with someone; it's that you fully understand him, emotionally and intellectually'.

Habit 6: Synergize

Synergy got a bad press when it was used as the logic for overpriced acquisition strategies. The acquisition of HBOS, it was claimed, would give Lloyds 'crucial advantages in funding costs and synergies' and made 'clear sense' for Lloyds. Such was the view in September 2008, but three years later such benefits were less than evident. But Covey uses synergy in the sense that creative cooperation – the principle that the whole is greater than the sum of its parts – encourages us to 'see the good and potential in the other person's contribution'. Developing this habit can produce a steady flow of 2+2 = 5+ type results.

Habit 7: Sharpen the saw

Covey illustrates this by telling a story supposing that you come upon a man in the woods sawing down a tree. 'You look exhausted!' you exclaim. 'How long have you been at it?' 'Over five hours,' he replies, 'and I am beat. This is hard.' 'Maybe you could take a break for a few minutes and sharpen that saw. Then the work would go faster.' 'No time,' the man says emphatically. 'I'm too busy sawing.' Habit 7 is taking time to sharpen the saw (you're the saw). It's the habit of self-renewal that makes all the others possible. Covey interprets the self into four parts: the spiritual, mental, physical and the social/emotional, which all need feeding and developing.

How real companies use Covey's concepts

The concepts behind the seven habits appear to be a superior and cerebral take on time management, so much so that in 1997 Covey joined forces with Franklin Quest Co, a leading provider of time management training seminars and products. The new business, Franklin Covey Co, is quoted on the New York Stock Exchange and has as clients 82 of the Fortune 100 companies and more than two-thirds of the Fortune 500 companies, as well as thousands of other companies and governmental agencies at all levels. The 'seven habits' approach has attracted corporations such as AT&T, Deloitte & Touche, Saturn, Ford, Marriott, Xerox, Merck, Dow Chemical, the Army Corps of Engineers, and the Department of Energy, to name just a few. The dominant premise of the book is that to become more effective you need to change your attitude to events. You can either complain about the things you don't like in your life or you can set about changing them. Not surprisingly, this has been adopted as a generic model for every subject from personal finance to marriage guidance.

How it dovetails with other guru theories

In preparation for writing *7 Habits*, Covey read all the success literature published in the US since 1776: hundreds of books, articles, and essays on self-improvement and popular psychology. He noticed that 'almost all the writings that helped build our country in its first 150 years or so identified character as the foundation of success'. The literature of what we might call the 'character ethic' helped Americans cultivate integrity, humility, fidelity, temperance, courage, justice, patience, industry. Compared with the early success literature, the writings of the last 50 years may seem superficial – filled with social-image consciousness, technique, and quick fixes. There, the solutions derive not from the character ethic, but the personality ethic.

What sets Covey apart is that his work is a holistic and accessible approach to the seemingly intractable field of changing habits, for the better. His ideas build on those developed by experts across a wide spectrum of related concepts. Peter Drucker's *Effective*

Executive (1966), focusing on 'how to allocate time because you can get more of almost any resource except time', is relevant to habit 3. The Johari window model, devised by American psychologists Joseph Luft and Harry Ingham in 1955, also referred to as a 'disclosure/feedback model of self awareness', applies to Covey's ideas on habit 5. Kurt Lewin, a German-born professor at the Massachusetts Institute of Technology (MIT) has his work on group dynamics and how change can be best effected in organizations used to support Covey's ideas on habit 6. In 1943 in an article entitled 'Defining the Field at a Given Time' published in the *Psychological Review*, Lewin described what is now known as force field analysis. Covey breaks this down into restraining forces: negative, emotional, illogical, unconscious and social/psychological; and driving forces: positive, reasonable, logical, conscious and economic.

Validity today

Covey's ideas have stood the test of time, and in any event he doesn't claim any particular right to his ideas, saying: 'Actually I did not invent the seven habits, they are universal principles and most of what I wrote about is just common sense. I am embarrassed when people talk about the Covey habits, and dislike the idea of being some sort of guru.' Covey has added an eighth habit for which he has written a 352-page book devoted exclusively to the subject of 'from effectiveness to greatness'. Tapping into greatness, Covey claims, 'is a matter of finding the right balance of four human attributes: talent, need, conscience and passion' in order to move beyond effectiveness into the realm of greatness.

Covey's work is certainly not rocket science, but using everyday examples of how people have improved their lives by adopting changed habits, he provides a route map to success.

Peter Drucker

By Colin Barrow

Name: Peter F Drucker

Born: 1909; **died:** 2005

Expertise: Management consultancy

Known for: The concept of management by objectives (MBO)

Best-known title: *The Practice of Management* (1954)

Who is Peter Drucker?

Drucker is credited with turning management into a profession akin to that of the scientist or medical doctor. Educated in Austria and England, Drucker became a financial reporter for *Frankfurter General Anzeiger* in 1929. Always seen as an outsider, more writer than academic, his skill as a journalist made his work more accessible than the more usual business school tomes.

Drucker left Germany in 1933, first going to England, then going on to America in 1937 to work as a correspondent for a group of British newspapers. In 1939, Drucker took a part-time teaching position at Sarah Lawrence College in New York, giving him his first exposure to teaching, a vocation he was to pursue throughout his life, taking his last class in the spring of 2002. He joined the faculty of Bennington College in Vermont in 1942 as professor of politics and philosophy, where he had the opportunity to spend two years studying the management structure of General Motors.

His 39 books, ranging from *The End of the Economic Man* (1939) to his last *The Effective Executive in Action*, published posthumously in January 2006, co-authored with Joseph A Maciariello, have between them been translated into more than 30 languages.

What is Drucker known for?

His experience with GM led to the publication of the 'concept of the corporation', where Drucker introduced the concept of the decentralized organization using delegation, as opposed to command and control, to manage the enterprise. Despite its becoming a bestseller in both the US and Japan, GM largely ignored the lessons in this book, even going so far as to hint that owning a copy was not a career-enhancing strategy. It did, however, launch Drucker's career as a management consultant par excellence.

In 1950 Drucker went to the New York University's Graduate School of Business, where he taught until 1971 and by his own reckoning did his best work. First among many compelling works was his 1954 book *The Practice of Management*, with chapter headings such as 'What is a Business?' and 'Managing Growth', designed to appeal to practicing executives. In this book he introduced and popularized the idea of 'management by objectives', without actually using that term. John Tarrant, Drucker's biographer, noted that Drucker once said he had first heard the term MBO used by Alfred Sloan, author of *My Years with General Motors*, a book that didn't come out until 1963, over a decade after Drucker's.

He called the process 'management by objectives and self-control' and his student, the late George S Odiorne, used *Management Decisions by Objectives* as the title for a book published in 1969. However, MBO is the name that has stuck, spawning a host of imitators and embellishers whilst holding firm to its central tenet. Drucker identified five fundamental principles of management: organizing, motivating, communicating, establishing measurements of performance and developing people, all around agreed objectives.

The concepts

The concepts advanced in support of MBO and much of Drucker's other writing were based on the following beliefs.

1. A company's primary responsibility is to serve its customers, not simply to make a profit. Nevertheless profit is essential if the business is to survive. So a business should be managed by balancing a variety of needs and goals, rather than a single value.

2. Drucker saw employees as assets rather than a cost, claiming them to be an organization's most valuable resource. He was amongst the first to use the term 'knowledge worker', identifying them as central to success in a progressive economy. A manager's job is to give people the tools to perform. Drucker believed that 'great companies could stand among humankind's noblest inventions'. But to achieve this they had to understand the aspirations, needs and responsibilities of their workforces and the communities in which they had to operate.

3. Decentralization, Drucker believed, was a better way to run an organization than the old command and control model with orders being given down the chain of command. He was an early advocate of de-layering organization.

4. Simplification, Drucker saw as a virtue that many corporations had lost. Firms tend to produce too many products, build departments doing work that should really be outsourced and expand into sectors that they don't really understand. Drucker posed three questions, whose answers would keep any organization firmly pointed in the right direction. These now form the classic opening discussion for a management consultant's first client meeting and are the yardstick against which every objective should be measured.

   a. What is our business?
   b. Who is our customer?
   c. What does our customer consider valuable?

5. The need for 'planned abandonment'. Businesses share a human failing in wanting to trumpet 'yesterday's achievements'

rather than seeing when they are no longer useful and letting go. Drucker recommended that at regular intervals, say every three years or so, an organization should rigorously examine every function, product, service, process, technology and market and prune out the inevitable deadwood.

6. Drucker believed that taking action without thinking is the cause of every failure. Thinking he saw as a function of leadership, and whilst management is doing things right, leadership is doing the right things.

7. Asking the right questions, Drucker saw as the defining skill of a great manager. This pithy quote sums up his views: 'the important and difficult job is never to find the right answer, it is to find the right question. For there are few things as useless – if not as dangerous – as the right answer to the wrong question.'

Management by objectives (MBO) was seen by Drucker as having five key stages, as set out in the figure opposite.

The first stage is to provide employees with a clear understanding of their roles and responsibilities as well as the results they are expected to achieve. Drucker saw the leader's main task as defining the mission and vision for the organization. Without absolute clarity at this stage no-one working there will be clear either. Drucker identified three big advantages for the organization by starting the process in this way.

● Involving employees in the goal-setting process increases employee empowerment, job satisfaction and commitment to achieving the objectives.

● Understanding how their activities relate to the achievement of the organization's goal makes it easier for people to see where and why they need to cooperate.

● Higher levels of management can make certain that their subordinates are all rowing in the agreed direction.

Management by objectives

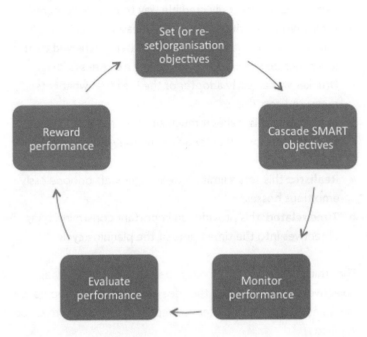

Cascading the organization's objectives to those responsible for achieving them is the second stage of MBO. Cascading, though it is the word used, is not quite the meaning of the process. However, it is self-evident that if an organization's mission is to be achieved everyone on the payroll has to work in some way to that end. But in order to make the process effective Drucker determined that the goals that were agreed should be attainable and answerable. The acronym SMART, though not specifically mentioned in *The Practice of Management*, is certainly there in spirit. He indicated that the cascade should work in practice, including the following elements.

- **Specific:** Drucker was against ambiguous goals, as having clear goals was the only credible way to monitor progress.
- **Measurable:** activities that can be measured, such as sales targets, have a better chance of being achieved than less concrete goals, such as improving a business's image. Drucker was an early adopter of the idea that what gets measured gets done.
- **Achievable:** this makes it much easier to get buy-in when the person responsible for achieving the goal has a hand in developing it.
- **Realistic:** this sets a limit on over-eager staff or hopelessly ambitious bosses.
- **Time related:** this provides an important constraint, tying objectives into the time frame of the planning cycle.

The third stage is to monitor performance against agreed objectives. This reinforces the idea that objectives should be measurable and that a system to report against them must be in place.

The fourth stage is to evaluate performance against the agreed objectives. This is a critical element, as clearly some elements of performance are outside the control of even the most able, dedicated and committed individuals. The assumptions on which the objectives depend come into play here. So if, for example, the organization assumes the economy will grow, and a major credit crunch drags the world into recession, then the original objectives may reasonably fail the test of being realistic.

The fifth stage is built around the idea that whilst what gets measured gets done, what gets rewarded gets done again. Then the organization goes back round the cycle, setting new objectives for the next time period.

How real companies use Drucker's concepts

MBO has been used successfully by businesses around the world. Although Drucker was persona non grata at General Motors, MBO was very much part of the culture in hundreds of other big American corporations and tens of thousands of other businesses, and not just in the US. Drucker had a big following in Japan, where his views on the corporation as more than simply a profit generator, but as a community built on trust and respect for employees, struck a chord. MBO's big break came in 1957 when it was declared to be an integral part of 'The HP Way', the much-praised management philosophy of Hewlett-Packard, a phenomenally successful computer company that posted net revenue of $126.3bn in 2010, up from $115bn in 2009.

Dave Packard, who with Bill Hewlett founded HP, said of MBO in his 1995 book *How Bill Hewlett and I Built the Company*:

> **No operating policy has contributed more to Hewlett-Packard's success ... MBO ... is the antithesis of management by control. The latter refers to a tightly controlled system of management of the military type ... Management by objectives, on the other hand, refers to a system in which overall objectives are clearly stated and agreed upon, and which gives people the flexibility to work toward those goals in ways they determine best for their own areas of responsibility.**

In a comprehensive review of 30 years of research on the impact of management by objectives, ('Impact of management by objectives on organizational productivity', R Rodgers, JE Hunter, *Journal of Applied Psychology*, 76(2), Apr 1991, 322–336), 68 of the 70 studies showed productivity gains, and only two studies showed losses. The authors concluded that companies whose CEOs demonstrated high commitment to MBO showed, on average, a 56% gain in productivity. Even in companies with CEOs who showed only lukewarm commitment there was a 6% gain in productivity.

How it dovetails with other guru theories

Drucker freely admitted that he did not invent management by objectives, drawing heavily on the work of American engineer Frederick Winslow Taylor (circa 1911) and others. Taylor is credited with coining the phrase 'time is money' and was one of the pioneers of the search for the 'one best way' to execute such basic managerial functions as selection, promotion, compensation, training and production. Taylor was followed by Henri Fayol (1919), a successful managing director of a French mining company, who developed what he called the 14 principles of management, recognizing that his list was neither exhaustive nor universally applicable. He also set out what he saw as the five primary functions of a manager. Nearly a decade later, Luther Gulick, an American, and Lydnall Urwick, a founder of the British management consultancy profession, expanded Fayol's list to seven executive management activities summarized by the acronym POSDCORB.

- Planning
- Organizing
- Staffing
- Directing
- Co-ordinating
- Reporting
- Budgeting

Drucker's talent lay in building on these ideas and turning them into language and procedures that managers could understand and use.

Validity today

MBO for most managers today is more likely to mean management buy-out than management by objectives. This would certainly not have given the master much pleasure. When acquisitive conglomerates were all the rage he crusaded against reckless mergers. But Drucker himself never saw MBO as a cure-all, stating, 'Management by objectives works if you know the objectives: 90% of the time you don't.'

Today's managers would be more familiar with more complicated business tools doing much the same things. The most obvious successor to MBO is the balanced scorecard developed by Robert Kaplan and David Norton. It was introduced in a *Harvard Business Review* article in 1992 as 'a management process that sets out to align business activities to the vision and strategy of the organization, improve internal and external communication and monitor organization performance against strategic goals'. Nothing here that Drucker would disagree with. Drucker's philosophy was that management is a liberal art, 'it deals with people, their values, their growth and development, social structure, the community and even with spiritual concerns ... the nature of humankind, good and evil'. These issues look like being around for a while yet.

Tim Ferriss

By Robert Craven

Name: Timothy Ferriss

Born: 1977

Expertise: Entrepreneurship, writing, public speaking and investment

Known for: Writing the *4-Hour Workweek*, successful investments in technology companies and health and fitness activities

Best-known titles: *The 4-Hour Workweek: Escape 9–5, Live Anywhere and Join the New Rich* (2007); *The 4-Hour Body* (2010)

Who is Tim Ferriss?

Tim Ferriss is an American entrepreneur, public speaker and author. He describes his teachings as 'lifestyle design', applying the Pareto principle and Parkinson's Law to business and personal life.

Before publication of *The 4-Hour Workweek*, Ferriss was largely unknown to the public, but his book has changed all that. In the book he challenges people's fundamental assumptions about how they live their lives: he appears as a living case study. Through his application of the principles and techniques proposed in the book he hit the *New York Times* and *Wall Street Journal* bestseller lists.

What is Ferriss known for?

Ferriss is known for applying his ology to give himself 'the luxury lifestyle'. His book shows readers how they too can follow a step-by-step process to do the same. Ferriss, aged 23, set up Brain-Quicken, a sports nutrients company, and subsequently sold it in 2009 to a London-based private equity firm. He holds the *Guinness Book of Records* world record for the most consecutive tango spins in one minute; he became the national champion in the 1999 USAWKF Sandshoe (Chinese kick-boxing) championship; in 2008 he won *Wired* magazine's 'Greatest Self-Promoter of all time' prize and was named as one of *Fast Company*'s 'Most Innovative Business People of 2007'.

The 4-Hour Workweek was published in 2007. The book was a manifesto for the mobile lifestyle and Ferriss was the ideal ambassador. In a world of increasing technological complexity he advocates using the available tools (that usually tend to actually complicate things) to become more effective and filling your personal time with the things you really want to have. Clinical goal-setting meets time management and effectiveness in the real world!

The concepts

The book offers a step-by-step guide to 'luxury lifestyle design'.

The back cover states: 'Do not read this book unless you want to quit your job: Forget the old concept of retirement and the rest of the deferred-life plan – there is no reed to wait and every reason not to.'

Ferriss uses the acronym DEAL to describe the four main chapters, standing for:

- Definition
- Elimination
- Automation
- Liberation.

D is for definition

Ferriss turns misguided common sense upside down and 'introduces rules and objectives of the new game'. He replaces self-defeating assumptions and explains concepts such as relative wealth and eustress (beneficial stress). The focus is on figuring out what a person really wants, getting over fears, seeing beyond society's past 'expectations' and figuring out what it will really cost to get to where the person wants to actually go. This section explains a lifestyle recipe before adding the next three ingredients.

E is for elimination

Ferriss 'kills the obsolete notion of time management'. The Pareto principle (80/20 rule) is applied to focus on those tasks that contribute the majority of the benefit: increase per-hour results tenfold with counter-intuitive 'new rich' techniques such as cultivating selective ignorance, developing a low-information diet and generally ignoring the unimportant. Parkinson's Law is applied to limit the actual amount of time spent working on a task. The challenge is to be clear about the difference between efficiency and effectiveness – and *The 4-Hour Workweek* is all about effectiveness. This section of the book provides the first of the three luxury lifestyle design ingredients: time.

A is for automation

Creating and building a sustainable, automatic source of income. A turnkey, repeatable system. Using geographical arbitrage, outsourcing and rules of non-decision, Ferriss puts cash flow on autopilot. Techniques included are drop-shipping, automation, Google Adwords, Adsense and outsourcing. This section provides the second ingredient of the luxury lifestyle design: income.

L is for liberation

The successful automation of one's life and the liberation from the geographical location and job. The idea of 'mini-retirements' is promoted as an alternative to the 'deferred life' career path where people work their 9–5 until they get to retirement in their 60s, when they are too old to enjoy all that the world has to offer and ambition and enthusiasm has been diminished. This is the mobile manifesto: concepts such as flawless remote control and escaping the boss are introduced. Liberation is not about cheap travel but about breaking the bonds that confine the person to a single location (if the reader has a 'regular' job then the order of the steps should be DELA). This section delivers the third and final ingredient for the luxury lifestyle design: mobility.

Ferriss asserts that technology such as email, instant messaging, internet-enabled PDAs and other handheld mobile devices actually complicate most lives rather than simplify them. At the time this was a revolutionary reaction to the clamor around the latest 'time-saving' technologies. He advocates hiring virtual assistants (from developing countries) to free up personal time.

He concedes 'much of what I recommend will seem impossible and even offensive to basic common sense – I expect that'. Statements such as 'everything popular is wrong ... be unreasonable ... cultivate selective ignorance, interrupt interruptions, management by absence, filling the void: adding life after subtracting work, these are scary challenges for some.

His assertion that you can achieve whatever you want but most people don't know what they really want in the first place is one that has liberated some readers but threatened the basic assumptions that others have had. He is, and it is, not everyone's cup of tea!

The thesis is a blueprint for freelance, independent thinking and living.

How real companies use Ferriss' concepts

Ferriss is his own best case study: a self-confessed self-publicist who wins awards for his art. His books and blogs positively brag about how he has succeeded by using the very tools he advises others to use.

Ferriss is the best-known exponent of the 'new rich' lifestyle and there are now entire communities following similar principles of living the life of an ultravagabond.

The 4-Hour Workweek book, blog and associated website (which contains bonus chapters) give numerous examples and mini-case studies, such as:

- **How to Get $700,000 of Advertising for $10,000**
- **How to Learn Any Language in 3 Months.**

They also provide templates and an online round-the-world trip planner. He not only talks about what to do but he also shows you how to do it.

In the book, Ferriss tells how he went from $40,000 per year and 80 hours per week to $40,000 per month and four hours per week, how blue-chip escape artists travel the world without quitting their jobs and how to eliminate 50% of your work in 48 hours.

For freelance, independent business owners, *The 4-Hour Workweek* manifesto is really an extension of Gerber's E-Myth. What Ferriss succeeds in doing is getting anyone in business to challenge whether there is a simpler, more effective technique for them to get out of their business what they really want. The book rattles cages and tends to haunt people till they either ignore the call for freedom or start to take on some of Ferriss' key ideas.

How it dovetails with other guru theories

Ferriss is like Michael Gerber (on small business design and automation) plus Stephen Covey (on goals and effectiveness) ... on steroids.

He openly acknowledges his major influences as David Schwartz (*The Magic of Thinking Big*), Dan S Kennedy (*How to Make Millions with Your Ideas*), Michael E Gerber (*The E-Myth Revisited*) and Ralph Potts (*Vagabonding: An Uncommon Guide to the Art of Long-Term World Travel*). His work has influenced a wave of recent authors but, more importantly, he has challenged the old school assumptions and so his influence will be felt long after he has gone.

Validity today

A recent author, there had always been a question about whether Ferriss was 'all sizzle and no steak', whether his work was a triumph of style over substance. Business schools find it hard to celebrate an unashamed self-help book. His unscientific approach has been forgiven because of the exuberance and enthusiasm that he writes with. And if attitude is such an important attribute then *The 4-Hour Workweek* certainly challenges how people do things. The publication of his second book, *The 4-Hour Body* (2010), received more conflicting reviews, despite its bestseller status.

Ferriss has never denied being a self-publicist; he openly and willingly admits to it. *The 4-Hour Workweek* arrived on the book scene like a breath of fresh air when most contemporary books were over-pompous or over-complicating simple ideas. He told a great personal story, demonstrating proofs and evidence that his blueprint can work. For many *The 4-Hour Workweek* and its associated literature has become a lifestyle choice.

Michael George

By Colin Barrow

Name: Michael L George

Born: 1963

Expertise: Lean six sigma, a groundbreaking management methodology

Known for: Reducing the costs associated with operating business, government and more recently military processes. He is a leading champion of the lean six sigma (LSS) process

Best-known titles: *Lean Six Sigma: Combining Six Sigma Quality with Lean Production Speed* (2002); *Lean Six Sigma for Service: How to Use Lean Speed and Six Sigma Quality to Improve Services and Transactions* (2003); *Fast Innovation: Achieving Superior Differentiation, Speed to Market, and Increased Profitability* (2005)

Who is Michael George?

George holds a BS in Physics from the University of California, an MS in Physics from the University of Illinois as well as the rights to a number of US patents in the waste reduction field. His first book, *America Can Compete*, set out his stall as a champion of the US fight against competition from Japan. Since then his ideas have inspired a veritable A–X of American corporates from Abbot Laboratories, through Apple, Ford, GE and Microsoft right through to Xerox.

George began his career at Texas Instruments in 1964. In 1969, he founded the venture startup International Power Machines, took the company public, and subsequently sold it to a division of Rolls-Royce. This provided the resources to enable him to study the Toyota Production System and TQM at first hand in Japan in 1986. There he uncovered the secret of Japanese manufacturing success, which led George to embark on a mission to help US companies become competitive with the Japanese in cost, quality and production-to-delivery cycle time.

What is George known for?

George developed the lean six sigma (LSS) methodology, combining two already well-established initiatives, lean production and six sigma, into one integrated program (see figure overleaf). The former is an approach ascribed to Toyota, where it sought to eliminate or continuously reduce waste, described as anything that doesn't add value. Lean enabled Toyota to rise from its foundations in 1933 as the automobile department of its principal business, manufacturing weaving looms, to the world's largest automotive manufacturing enterprise. Six sigma was the result of work at Motorola in the 1970s. The company discovered that, contrary to its previously held views, increasing quality actually resulted in lower costs rather than higher. Raising quality reduced related expense for repairs, refunds and loss of corporate image, so any costs associated with raising quality were more than compensated for. Motorola has documented more than $16bn in savings as a result of its six sigma initiatives.

George founded his consultancy, The George Group, to promulgate his ideas, and his books provided a step-by-step roadmap for profiting from the best elements of lean and six sigma, initially in the manufacturing arena, to which he later added the service sectors. He built the group to a business with revenues of $120m per year and 300 employees, selling to Accenture in 2007. He is a founder member of Strong America, a not for profit organization dedicated to alerting people to the danger of the US's ever-increasing national debt. His new mission is to save the US from financial disaster, the subject of his latest book *SOS! Our Economy is Sinking!*

Lean six sigma

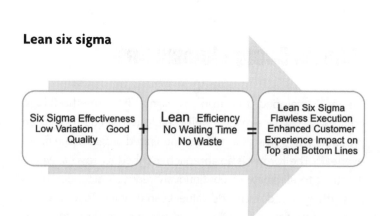

The concepts

Lean six sigma incorporates the speed and impact of lean with the quality and variation control of six sigma. The roots of LSS stem from the thinking behind six sigma itself, which in a nutshell is about getting it right 99.99966% of the time! First you have to grasp the central limit theorem, which states that the mean of a sample of a large population will approach 'normal' as the sample gets bigger. The most valuable feature here is that even quite small samples are normal. The Bell Curve, also called the Gaussian distribution after Johann Gauss (1777–1855), shows how far values are distributed around a mean, the central point of the data. The distribution is measured in standard deviations, that is, their distance from the mean, and it is this that makes it possible to state how accurate a sample is likely to be. Opinion polls predicting elections based on samples as small as 1,000 are usually reliable within four percentage points, 19 times out of 20.

The normal distribution curve showing standard deviations

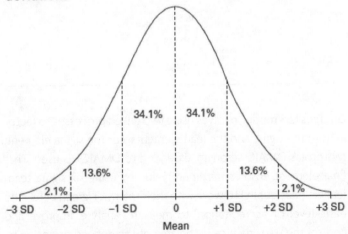

The figure on the previous page is a normal distribution that shows that 68.2% of the observations of a normal population will be found within one standard deviation (also known as one sigma, Greek for the letter 's') of the mean, 95.5% within two standard deviations, and 99.7% within three standard deviations. So almost 100% of the observations will be observed in a span of six standard deviations, three below the mean and three above the mean, hence the term 'six sigma'. Motorola's executives believed that if their distributions had six of these sigma from the mean to the limit of their quality specification, they would essentially have virtually no failures due to quality standards (see table below).

Likely defects at six sigma

Percentage of successful outputs or operations	Defects per million opportunities (DPMO)	'Process sigma'
99.99966	3.4	6
99.98	233	5
99.4	6,210	4
93.3	66,807	3
69.1	308,538	2
30.9	691,462	1

George's LSS model involves using two linked processes to factor in both the sigma and the lean elements. For the sigma element, Motorola's DMAIC acronym, extended to DMAICT is used. That final element ensures maximum value by using six sigma team leaders (black belts) to work with their teams of 'green belts' (the basic level of accreditation) to measure, analyse, improve and control the performance in the area of the defined opportunity.

- Define opportunity
- Measure performance
- Analyse opportunity
- Improve performance
- Control performance
- Transfer best practice to other areas.

The central thinking behind lean is to manage the lead (also referred to as the cycle time), that is, the length of time required for an organization to deliver a good or service to a customer to their required standard from the time that they initiate their requirement. The shorter this lead/cycle time, the less the cost, as stockholding, days waiting for payment and other non-value-added costs will be eliminated. There are two approaches to shortening lead time:

- reduce the number of stages in the process
- increase the average completion rate for the items.

George advances three key lean tools to help eliminate waste and reduce lead time in the process.

- Value add versus non-value add analysis: this essentially involves asking the 'customer' what they value enough in the process to pay for. The aim here is to identify and eliminate waste that drives up the cost of the product or service, and reduce errors by simplifying the process, and create additional capacity. For example a courier service could operate a delivery tracking system telling customers to within one hour when their package would arrive. But if the customer will be at home for several hours anyway, delivering that service will result in a non-value cost.
- Program 5S stands for sort, set in order, shine, standardize, and sustain. This is a methodology for organizing, cleaning,

developing and sustaining a productive work environment. Improve safety, develop ownership of workspace, improve productivity and improve maintenance. Fundamentally this process empowers work teams to become more efficient.

- Value stream mapping: this is a graphical tool to help you see and understand the flow of the material and accompanying information as a product or service makes its way through to completion. Basically this is an application of CPA (critical path analysis, see figure below). The steps in the process are as follows:

  - identify the events
  - decide on the sequence in which they must be carried out
  - draw the network. Calculate the completion time for each event
  - identify the longest and hence critical path
  - keep the chart updated as events unwind.

Using critical path analysis for value stream mapping

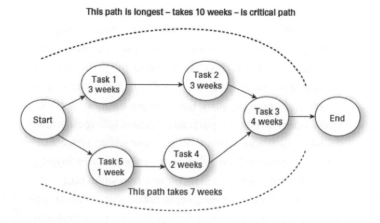

This path is longest – takes 10 weeks – is critical path

Task 1
3 weeks

Task 2
3 weeks

Start

Task 3
4 weeks

End

Task 5
1 week

Task 4
2 weeks

This path takes 7 weeks

In the example in the figure opposite, as tasks 4 and 5 don't lie on the critical path, any cost associated with speeding them up would be of no value.

How real companies use George's concepts

If sales of George's books are anything to go by almost every major company has had some exposure to lean six sigma. Now a global brand business tool, LSS is as much a philosophy or vision as it is a metric or methodology. Clients of the George Group included Caterpillar, Xerox, Honeywell/Allied Signal, ITT and United Technologies.

In 2004, the US Navy selected the George Group to use the lean six sigma method to reduce costs and cycle time while also improving quality. The US Army followed suit, eliminating waste and reporting $14bn in savings.

In 2001 Hubbell Incorporated, a Fortune 1000 company, embarked on a lean six sigma program led by Timothy H Powers, the company's president and CEO. Hubbell, incorporated in 1905, is primarily engaged in the design, manufacture and sale of quality electrical and electronic products for a broad range of construction, industrial and utility applications. Products are either sourced complete, manufactured, or assembled by subsidiaries in the US, Canada, Switzerland, Puerto Rico, Mexico, China, Italy, the UK, Brazil and Australia. Although a strong and successful company, its key numbers were moving in the wrong direction. Within three years that trend had been reversed.

- Net sales up 35% compared to an 8% decline in the preceding year.
- Net income up 138% compared to a 65% decline in the preceding year.
- Earnings per share up 132% compared to a 64% decline in the preceding year.
- Inventory reduced by $170m despite sales being up by over a third.

In his 2003 annual report, Powers acknowledged the value of LSS, 'We began a "lean transformation" of our company and culture. Almost immediately, we saw improvement we could not have generated otherwise.' In his 2010 annual report Powers confirmed his company's continued commitment to the principles that underpin the LSS initiative: 'Over the years, Hubbell has made tremendous strides in productivity, and there has been and will be no let up. The company continues hammering away to reduce cost – while simultaneously improving customer service and satisfaction.' Over the 12 months to December 2010, a challenging period in the company's business sectors, sales turnover was up 8%, profit by 21% and earnings per share by 14%.

How it dovetails with other guru theories

The foundations of LSS derive from a cross-section of long-established theories, starting with the work of Frederick W Taylor. Usually referred to as the 'father of scientific management', he studied and measured the way people worked, searching out ways to improve productivity. His book, *The Principles of Scientific Management* (1911), showed how science could replace apprenticeship as the way to transfer knowledge about how tasks should be done.

The next advance in the discipline took place with the introduction of mathematical models used during World War II to make maximum use of scarce resources. Tasks such as removing bottlenecks in tank production led to dramatic increases in output. Henry Gantt, a mechanical engineer, management consultant and associate of Frederick Taylor, showed how an entire process could be described in terms of both tasks and the time required to carry them out. He developed what became known as the Gantt chart. By laying out the information on a grid with tasks on one axis and their time sequence along the other it was possible to see at a glance an entire production plan and potential bottlenecks.

W Edwards Deming, an American statistician, is considered as the founder of modern quality management. He enhanced the inspection aspect of quality control with the introduction of statistical probability techniques. His view was that quality should be designed into products and processes and that mass inspection was redundant, as statistical sampling using control charts will signal when a process is out of control.

In Deming's 14-point 'system of profound knowledge' he explains that becoming a quality-driven organization requires everyone, starting with top management, 'to fully embrace a new way of thinking that involves seeking the greater good for everyone involved and implementing continuous improvement'. Deming's ideas were adopted enthusiastically by the Japanese after World War II. It was not until the Japanese motor industry was cutting deep into its home market that US industry woke up to Deming's message on quality. The rush was on to introduce a host of initiatives to re-galvanize American industry and, by extension, Western industry. JIT (just in time), TQM (total quality management), quality circles and six sigma were rushed into service, with LSS being the latest and perhaps the most successful variant.

Validity today

If Google Trend's estimate of world interest in lean six sigma is anything to go by, interest in the concept is as strong as ever (see figure below). LSS shot to prominence in 2004 and has remained strong ever since. The countries showing the greatest level of interest are Singapore and India, with the US lying in fifth place and the UK in eighth.

Google trends results for lean sigma six

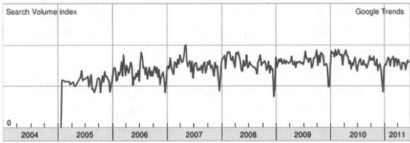

Michael Gerber

By Gerard Burke

Name: Michael E Gerber

Born: 1936

Expertise: Small business growth and entrepreneurism

Best known for: The idea of entrepreneurs working *on* their business, rather than *in* it

Best-known titles: *The E-Myth Revisited: Why Most Small Businesses Don't Work and What to Do About It* (1995); *Awakening the Entrepreneur Within: How Ordinary People Can Create Extraordinary Companies* (2008); *The E-Myth Enterprise – How to Turn a Great Idea into a Thriving Business; The Most Successful Small Business in the World* (2010)

Who is Michael Gerber?

Michael E Gerber has been called the small business guru. He founded E-Myth Worldwide, the coaching, training and education firm, in 1977, to help small businesses develop. He teaches small business owners to work *on* their business, rather than *in* it, and believes that anyone can be taught to create a successful company.

What is Gerber known for?

Gerber is the author of 13 business books, including the bestselling E-Myth books. These books argue that most small businesses are not started by entrepreneurs, but by 'technicians' suffering from an 'entrepreneurial seizure'. They create a business that looks like their old job; they have the technical skills but not the business skills. Gerber's idea was to teach these technicians business skills; and then teach them how to take a step back from the everyday operation of their business to focus more on overall strategy.

More recently, Gerber has focused on the special needs of entrepreneurs in the start-up phase. He argues that anyone can become an entrepreneur and create a successful company, a departure from the conventional wisdom on the question of whether entrepreneurs are born or made. Using a framework he calls the Dreaming Room, Gerber identifies four dimensions of the entrepreneurial personality, and recommends a 16-step pathway to invent and develop a small business.

The concepts

The concept of working on the business rather than in the business has become a central plank of nearly every development program or coaching approach designed to help owner-managers grow their businesses. The transition from working *in* the business all of the time to working *on* the business for some of the time can be very difficult to make.

The key to becoming a strategist, however, is to let go. As Gerber set out, the single biggest obstacle to the development of a business is the business owner's inability to do this. The owner needs to recognize that if they alone are the source of all power, decisions and leadership, then the business cannot grow beyond the limit of their resources. It's crucial to have a team in place to provide the launch pad for long-term growth. To let go of power, an owner must trust their team. But before they transfer powers to others, they must first have the confidence to let go emotionally.

The 'e-myth'

The myth of the entrepreneur or e-myth holds that people who go into business for themselves are not always entrepreneurs. Rather, Gerber calls them technicians suffering from 'entrepreneurial seizures'. These 'would-be entrepreneurs' make what Gerber calls a 'fatal assumption': they assume because they know how to do the technical work, that they know how to build a business.

The consultant creates a consultancy; the plumber starts a plumbing firm; the lawyer, a legal firm. But Gerber argues that these small companies cannot grow because their owners spend their time working *in* the business rather than doing what entrepreneurs do, which is to work *on* the business. They see the business as a job whereas an entrepreneur sees it as a product. Gerber's key realization was that would-be entrepreneurs run businesses that fail to fully achieve their potential because the owner doesn't truly know how to build a company that works without him or her.

In all Gerber's books, he writes about one underlying theme: three personalities reside inside every person (and, by extension, in every company). These are the entrepreneur, the manager, and the technician. The entrepreneur works at the enterprise level, the manager at the business level, and the technician at the practice level. Most people have an imbalance of the three personalities, with the technician usually dominant, and both the manager and entrepreneur undeveloped. It is this domination of the technician that Gerber believes keeps most small businesses from growing. The technician is limited by time and knowledge. There are only so many billable hours in the day, so the only way the technician can expand the business is by increasing the amount he's paid per hour. He calls this the 'tyranny of the expert'. Ultimately, the expert reaches a ceiling and can't go any further.

A technician runs a business limited by what he or she is able to do in the amount of time available. Adding support staff can help, but they eat up revenue. Usually there's enormous resistance to this, so the would-be entrepreneur is trapped in a prison of their own making. They had wanted independence and the opportunity to work at something they loved. But they do not feel liberated; they are more consumed than ever, and doing many more jobs than in the past.

On the other hand, the true entrepreneur knows that working *on* the business is absolutely essential. Then it can be built into a 'turnkey practice' that can be replicated. It's at this point that the entrepreneur begins to create a business. He or she has turned into a manager; a manager who will build a management system for a growing network of businesses. Those practices are replicable because, with a turnkey system, people with significantly less skill than the entrepreneur can perform just as well. The business becomes eight, 10, or 12 practices. That, says Gerber, is an enterprise; that's how to achieve growth.

The Dreaming Room™

Gerber believes that every single person has the ability to be creative. It is an instinct that we are born with, but that is not very developed. His mission, he says, is to awaken the entrepreneur within every single person that he comes into contact with. He suggests that anyone can learn the right way to create a successful business by overcoming common problems. Understanding markets and customers, securing capital, preparing financials – each element can be learned.

The essence of a business plan that always works is that it's not first and primarily about creating a business. Instead, it's about what the entrepreneur wants. This makes the process an exercise in creating objectives. Gerber urges entrepreneurs to look deeply at this question, otherwise they may suffer the fate of becoming successful at something they don't really want to do.

Gerber's advice to entrepreneurs is to dream continuously, passionately, with conviction, and not to be in a rush to know. From working with many businesses in the past 30 years, he had observed that what was missing was true invention and creativity; the entrepreneur as 'imaginer' or inventor.

So in December 2005, Gerber launched a new venture for entrepreneurs seeking to create world-class start-ups. Gerber leads two and a half day intensive courses throughout the US, Canada and the UK, aimed at guiding entrepreneurs to realize their dreams. Based on his experiences with entrepreneurs in the Dreaming Room™ events, Gerber wrote *Awakening The Entrepreneur Within – How Ordinary People Can Create Extraordinary Companies* in 2008.

The Awakening Entrepreneur™ is inspired by the belief that to truly flourish, a business must touch the lives of each of its four primary influencers – its customers, employees, suppliers and lenders and shareholders – in a deep and meaningful way. 'Awakened entrepreneurs' seek a path that has, at its core, a higher, more inspiring meaning than just making money, selling a product or seizing market share.

How real companies use Gerber's concepts

The problem of entrepreneurs working *in* the business rather than *on* it is so commonplace that the majority would recognize it. A good example of Gerber's 'technician' can be found in Ben Hillson, who started off as a happy artisan when he founded London-based events management business Aspect with fellow director Simon King-Cline. Back in the early days, they were at the heart of the creative and commercial processes of pitching to clients, creating visuals, and running events.

Several years of rapid growth followed. Ben and Simon were in great demand by their corporate clients and were personally required to oversee, and usually be present at, the events so that they could personally coach the CEOs and directors who would be speaking.

But by the end of 2009, all was not well, as Ben Hillson recalls: 'We were all working really hard and delivering some great stuff but the projects were smaller than we were used to, and we weren't seeing a return on our investment in sales.'

And on a personal level, Ben wasn't really enjoying the business as much as he used to. 'I knew I didn't want to carry on as I had before – working incredibly hard to generate new business, attend client meetings, organize events, and then trying to run the business in my spare time. Basically, I was a jack of all trades and master of none.' Part of the problem was rooted in Ben and Simon's 'meddling'. 'We had project teams with apparent autonomy, but we undermined them without realizing it by telling them how to do things and asking them to run everything past us.'

After a complete re-think of their approach, Ben and Simon encouraged the other members of the Aspect leadership team to develop and drive a short-term strategy for the business. Meanwhile, Ben and Simon focused on the long-term future of the business. 'Simon and I are no longer involved on an operational basis,' says Ben. 'We're preparing for the next stage of growth, which includes establishing stronger partnerships with clients and suppliers, and identifying potential acquisition targets. Ultimately, we're considering grooming the business for a sale or MBO.'

The Dreaming Room™ process has been taken up by owner-managers and those who train them. This is a recognition that many owner-managers need to be encouraged to take time to create a future they really want. Some choose to become a strategist and aim to be the next Richard Branson or Alan Sugar. And others choose to go back to doing the thing they love, and accept that they will never have a very big business. Both choices are fine since each enables the individual to create the future they want for their business and for themselves.

How it dovetails with other guru theories

McClelland identified that people have three types of needs: achievement, power and affiliation. He observed that entrepreneurs have the greatest need for achievement, and also that they are not motivated by money. This appears to match Gerber's observations that entrepreneurs are technicians working hard in their businesses but seemingly unable or unwilling to take decisions which would allow the business to develop.

Validity today

Just about every thinker, writer, business coach and training provider who works with small businesses and entrepreneurs has been influenced by Gerber's ideas. The e-myth is still one of the most powerful ideas in helping owner-managers and entrepreneurs meet the challenge of growing their businesses. The phrase 'working *on* the business rather than *in* it' is still quoted widely today just as Gerber first wrote it. It has been hugely influential.

As time has passed, the concept has been developed into models that allow for different stages of growth, such as the artisan-hero-meddler-strategist model. As a result, sophisticated programs and processes can now help owner-managers to make the transition between these stages.

Malcolm Gladwell

By Ditlev Bredahl

Name: Malcolm Gladwell

Born: 1963

Expertise: Business journalism; the link between individuals and social impact

Best known for: Empowering the reader to believe that real change is possible through the potentially epidemic implications of small-scale social events; unpicking the causes of epidemic social phenomena to understand why rapid, unexpected change takes place

Best-known titles: *The Tipping Point* (2000); *Blink* (2005); *Outliers* (2008); *What the Dog Saw: And Other Adventures* (2009)

Who is Malcolm Gladwell?

Malcolm Gladwell is the author of four critically acclaimed international bestsellers. Gladwell began his career as a business journalist with *The American Spectator* before moving to *The Washington Post*, and since 1996 has been a staff writer at the *New Yorker*. The influence of Gladwell's literary works has been recognized by *Time* magazine and *Newsweek*.

What is Gladwell known for?

Gladwell's first book, *The Tipping Point*, has sold over two million copies since it was published in 2000 and is still an influential publication. It analyses social phenomena in the context of business and brands to identify what causes trends to spiral into epidemics. *The Tipping Point* presents a set of rules business leaders can apply to assist in the recognition of the roles people play and the necessary conditions required to initiate social trends. Ultimately, it offered the first map for achieving exponential growth in sales.

Blink, Gladwell's second bestseller, offers a blueprint for improved decision making. *Blink* explores the notion of the adaptive unconscious and its ability to filter into small segments the vast quantity of information we process in order to come to sound decisions. Good judgement, or even gut instinct, is the 'X factor' in the success of many executives. Gladwell argues that spontaneous decisions, based on a 'thin slice' of subconscious information, are often as good as – or better than – decisions that are based on vast quantities of data and planning.

In *Outliers*, Gladwell's third work, he theorizes that '10,000 hours' is the rule for success, from Bill Gates to The Beatles.

The concepts

The key concept of *The Tipping Point* is that with the right combination of people and circumstance, it is possible to influence a trend which reaches, as Gladwell defines it, 'a moment of critical mass, the threshold, the boiling point', that triggers a social epidemic. *The Tipping Point* model states that ideas, products, messages and behavior can be made to spread like viruses by creating the right environment in accordance with three principal rules. The aim of the book is to show people how to start positive epidemics of their own, where only a little input (of the right kind) is required to enable it to spread quickly.

Rule 1: The law of the few

Gladwell stresses that social epidemics are driven by the efforts of a handful of exceptional people. These people exhibit one or more of three personality types – connectors, mavens and salesmen. The characteristics or social talents that enable these people to be successful are sociability, knowledge and the degree of influence they exert over their peers.

Connectors

These are people who are able to form a large network of friends and acquaintances. Connectors are the social glue that spread the message to others. Although connectors have the ability to help a trend become known, they are not always the innovators who make the initial discovery.

Mavens

The information supplier is known as a maven, a collector of information who is happy to share it with others. Mavens are motivated to help others gain knowledge, often in their own pursuit of information, which Gladwell notes is an effective way to get someone's attention. Mavens are the trusted sources of information others use to guide their opinions.

Salesmen

Salesmen persuade others to accept information. They are highly likeable, display powerful negotiation skills and have contagious or irresistible personalities. Other people want to agree with them, even if they may be initially unconvinced about the information that is presented.

The tipping point + the social media network

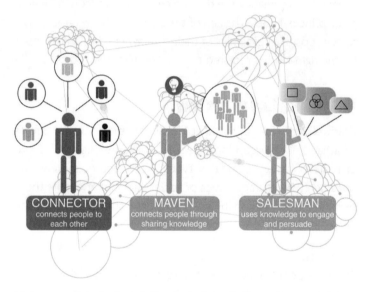

CONNECTOR
connects people to
each other

MAVEN
connects people through
sharing knowledge

SALESMAN
uses knowledge to engage
and persuade

(*Courtesy of Malcolm Gladwell, author of* The Tipping Point)

Rule 2: The stickiness factor

The 'stickiness factor' is what makes information memorable. A message, idea or product needs to be so memorable that it can create change and spur someone to action. According to Gladwell, the information age has created a stickiness problem. We suffer from too much clutter, and the result is that few of the ideas we are exposed to are practical or personal enough to stick. The key to finding stickiness is often not budget or the originality of an idea, but a small change to an existing or conventional idea that is already ingrained in our brains.

Rule 3: The power of context

'The power of context' addresses the role that the environment plays in reaching a tipping point. Along with the role played by unique individuals, and the nature of the trend itself, the likelihood that a trend will 'tip' also depends on the conditions and circumstances of the time and place in which it occurs.

Gladwell cites the 'broken windows' theory to explain how significant even an apparently minor environmental change can be to the success of a trend. The theory holds that crime and negative social epidemics in dilapidated neighborhoods can be reversed by tinkering with small details of the immediate environment, such as broken windows. In the simplest terms, a broken window demonstrates an apparent lack of concern about an area from its inhabitants and the authorities, offering an invitation to break more windows, which in turn leads to more serious misdemeanors and crime.

In Gladwell's view, group behavior is a function of social context and small changes can influence a positive overall environment that is conducive for trends to occur. Broken windows can tip normal levels of crime into an epidemic; fixing them can instigate a positive epidemic and a reduction in crime. Gladwell gives the example of a radical tip in crime rates in New York in the 1980s and 1990s. By focusing on apparently trivial issues, such as graffiti on trains, fare dodging and aggressive panhandling (begging), the authorities influenced the much bigger crime picture in a very positive way.

The audience too is contextual. Large numbers of people reinforce trends more quickly, and create a tipping point more effectively. However, it is not simply a case of 'the more, the merrier'; there is a ceiling on the number of people required. This is what Gladwell refers to as the 'rule of 150'. Put simply, 150 is the maximum number of people one is able to have a genuine social relationship with. Anthropological research has shown this to hold true in numerous societies throughout history, and the same can be seen in the military and many corporations. The right number of people creates a suitable social environment for a trend to tip, since the tipping point depends on the efficiency and intimacy of interpersonal relationships. Connectors, mavens and salesmen work as translators, adapting ideas and information into a language that the rest of the population will 'get'. These trend-setters then exploit their networks and peer influence to begin a chain reaction among other groups; the trigger point for an epidemic.

How real companies use Gladwell's concepts

Hush Puppies, the mid-1990s footwear fetish of the masses, is Gladwell's own case study of the tipping point concept in action. The crepe-soled shoe tipped from annual sales of 30,000 pairs in 1994, to over one million the following year. The influence of a handful of 'hipsters' – who, ironically, began wearing the shoes because nobody else did – in an environment with just the right kind of fashion consciousness, created a trend that tipped a tired brand into a household name, almost overnight.

LinkedIn, the world's largest social networking company for professionals, and Twitter, a real-time information network, are also examples of the tipping point in action. They are major influencers on the continued application of Gladwell's concept to businesses that want to instigate social epidemics. Social media channels collectively have created an environment where mavens, connectors and salesmen can create epidemic trends almost in real time. This is exactly what happens when a YouTube clip 'goes viral' or a topic is 'trending' on Twitter.

Within the internet hosting services and software business these concepts have proven themselves time and again. In 2007 I was on the team that founded VPS.NET, a company that offers cloud hosting services.

To launch the company, VPS.NET recruited likely salesmen to the cause by giving them access to the company's new cloud hosting service, free of charge. These people were not just good at convincing others, they were experts who would offer reasoned opinions and advice to other potential customers: they were also the company's mavens. Because forums and other social media were the places our customers hung out and talked about their service, VPS.NET quickly gained the volume of connections that propelled the company's trend towards its tipping point. Six months after launch, by 2010, VPS.NET had established a new market for mass-market cloud hosting services operating one of the world's five largest public clouds.

This success then created a new trend. Other hosting companies began to ask how they could license the technology the company had developed. The original sticky idea evolved to create a publicly available version of the company's software so that, just like VPS.NET, other hosting companies could bring cloud services to their share of the mass market. Software was given away free for the first year, increasing the stickiness. In doing so, VPS.NET recruited large numbers of hosting companies – again, a vocal, well-connected and expert community. These people became the salesmen, mavens and connectors.

How it dovetails with other guru theories

Gladwell's own influences for *The Tipping Point* include his mother, Joyce Gladwell, herself the published author of the novel *Brown Face, Big Master*. Her book explores the social and personal complications that people are faced with, a concept that Gladwell brought to his own writing in the context of business.

Social psychologist Stanley Milgram's 1967 study on 'six degrees of separation' found that, on average, six connections were required to deliver a letter to a stockbroker in Boston who was not known to the initial person in the chain. The study found that for half of the letters that arrived, just three friends of the stockbroker provided the final link in the chain. It was this fact that Gladwell focused on in *The Tipping Point*. He saw that certain types of people are key to the dissemination of information, which led to his 'law of the few'.

Many other authors and business leaders have built upon Gladwell's work. For example, Stephen Levitt and Stephen Dubner, the co-authors of *Freakonomics*, explore the idea that events that seem unrelated can actually be strongly connected, a theory that is closely linked to Gladwell's 'power of context' concept.

Validity today

The Tipping Point was published in 2000, some time before today's social networking trend had taken hold. Some of the book's detractors have argued that, because it predates the modern internet environment and particularly social networking, it must have limited value as it cannot describe the growth of trends and epidemics in this context.

This argument is extremely difficult to support. There is no better way to demonstrate the essential truths of *The Tipping Point* than by examining the way trends are created, rise and fall, either in, or because of, social networking sites such as Facebook, Twitter and LinkedIn.

The language may differ: 'trending', 'going viral' and so on – but the fundamental tipping point mechanics remain the same. In truth, social media are *The Tipping Point* writ large: our connectors on LinkedIn, the mavens we follow on Twitter, the salesmen in our Facebook friends list that introduce a new product, video or application; social media provide the context and the means to connect with influential people, enabling sticky ideas to thrive. The principal difference is time. Delivering a letter to an unknown stockbroker in the 1960s took days or weeks; the same process takes place almost immediately today.

Seth Godin

By Mark Roy

Name: Seth Godin

Born: 1960

Expertise: Named 'America's greatest marketer' by *American Way* magazine and the 'ultimate entrepreneur for the information age' by *Business Week*, Seth Godin is a bestselling author, a notable blogger and a renowned public speaker on marketing, direct marketing, new media and emerging trends

Known for: Pioneering the use of ethical direct marketing in the late 1990s, a practice Godin calls permission marketing

Best-known titles: *Permission Marketing: Turning Strangers Into Friends, and Friends Into Customers* (1999); *Purple Cow: Transform Your Business by Being Remarkable* (2003); *All Marketers Are Liars: The Power of Telling Authentic Stories in a Low-Trust World* (2005); *Small Is the New Big: and 193 Other Riffs, Rants, and Remarkable Business Ideas* (2006); *Tribes: We Need You to Lead Us* (2008); *Linchpin: Are You Indispensable?* (2011)

Who is Seth Godin?

Seth Godin is one of the most respected and influential thought leaders within marketing today. He has written 13 books on marketing, entrepreneurialism, bucking the trend, leadership and change, which have been translated into more than 30 languages. Many of the terms popularized in Godin's bestselling books have become part of marketing vernacular. In many ways ahead of their time, Godin's observations and ideologies have broken new ground and inspired change.

What is Godin known for?

After graduating from university in 1979, Godin pursued an MBA in Marketing at Stanford University and worked as a brand manager for a software company. After three years at Spinnaker Software, Godin left the company to launch a start-up book-packaging business, which he ran from his apartment in New York.

It was during this time that Godin launched a company called Yoyodyne, one of the first online marketing companies, which pioneered the use of ethical, permission-driven online marketing. A previously unknown concept, Godin's theories on 'anticipated, personal, and relevant' permission-based marketing formed the backbone of his most celebrated book, *Permission Marketing: Turning Strangers Into Friends, and Friends Into Customers*. In 1998, Yoyodyne was acquired by Yahoo! for a jaw-dropping $30m and Godin was appointed VP of direct marketing. However, after the publication of *Permission Marketing* in 1999 Godin's profile as an author and thought leader soared and he left Yahoo! in 2000 to pursue a full-time career as a writer and public speaker.

Marketing guru, orator, blogger, celebrated internet wunderkind, above all these things Seth Godin is best known for the concepts he expounds in his books and his unique approach to publishing and distributing them. Some might call his theorizing stating the obvious, but the fact of the matter is that when Godin tapped it out on his computer keys there was no manual; and any existing theory and practice just didn't translate to the new media age. To that end, Godin's hypotheses are not only influential but are constantly one step ahead of the curve and, as such, they have played an intrinsic part in molding the 'now'.

The concepts

Permission marketing, tribes, ideaviruses, purple cows, remarkable rifts, meatball sundaes and sneezers are just some of the concepts that Seth Godin has popularized through his books, but behind these catchy monikers there is a hefty dose of substance that hinges on a simple concept he introduced in his book *Permission Marketing*.

Godin's overarching belief is that marketing techniques that rely upon interrupting the consumer, such as TV and billboard advertising, are dead and that marketers don't have the leverage they once had to command the attention of an audience. Instead, he believes that power has transferred to the consumer and that marketers must have a respect for their increasingly savvy 'potential' audience. To succeed in our high traffic, media dominated world, marketers need to be transparent, honest and must work hard to engage their audience by delivering relevant, targeted and timely messages (and NOT SPAM) that the consumer wants to know about.

Always ahead of his time, Seth Godin believes that only the most remarkable ideas deserve to be spread (just like viruses) by 'sneezers', earning their right to popularity through merit alone. Today, with the proliferation of 'search', online social networking and video sharing this does seem rather obvious, but in 2000 when he released his third book, *Unleashing the Ideavirus*, Mark Zuckerberg was still at high school, YouTube was five years from formation and even internet super-giant Google Incorporated was in its infancy. Released online and free to download and share, *Unleashing the Ideavirus* is purported to be the most downloaded e-book of all time and proves Godin's theory that customers sharing content and marketing to each other works better than interrupting them.

Highly prolific in terms of his output, Godin's next two books *The Big Red Fez* (2002) and *Survival Is Not Enough* (2002) were released in the same year and became global bestsellers, firmly positioning him as one of the most influential business authors of the early noughties. Godin's light-footedness in responding to the problems of the moment gave his readers exactly what they needed: clear-headed solutions for surviving the boom and bust of the dotcom bubble and for getting the most out of their website, the demand for which was growing exponentially.

However, while these books were highly relevant and targeted it was his next book, *Purple Cow: Transform Your Business By Being Remarkable* (2003), which continued with themes developed in *Ideavirus* and *Permission Marketing* and gained similar recognition by becoming an immediate bestseller.

Like his previous titles, *Purple Cow* begins with the premise that old-age media marketing is defunct. He also asserts that marketing channels are saturated and our product needs have been satisfied. Therefore, to gain attention in a crowded environment, businesses need to create truly remarkable products (purple cows) and market them in remarkable ways. He proves his theory by showing practical examples of businesses that have achieved success in this manner and, being Godin, he took his *Purple Cow* to market in a highly innovative way. True to form, the book was initially self-published and sold online for just its shipping and handling charges, and came packaged in a purple milk carton!

In *Small Is the New Big: and 193 Other Riffs, Rants, and Remarkable Business Ideas* (2006), Godin looks at the benefits of being small in terms of measuring business success. His theory goes further by suggesting that being nimble and flexible in our fast-paced world (while thinking big) is a key ingredient in keeping ahead of the competition. Interestingly, the book is not as reactive as his previous titles and signals the diversification of his core theories from pure marketing to broader business/leadership strategy. To that end Godin's books *Tribes: We Need You to Lead Us* (2008) and *Linchpin: Are You Indispensable?* (2010) both take an in-depth look at professional evolution and leadership.

Ever keen to prove the relevance of his philosophies in a business setting, Godin launched an online community to promote *Tribes* and, instead of launching *Linchpin* using traditional media, he promoted it solely using social media by connecting with the online community to preview, review and feedback on his work.

A conceptualist at his core, Godin's remarkable ideas are not only reflected in his books, blogs and e-books but can also be seen in his unique brand of entrepreneurialism, which only serves to reinforce his message.

How real companies use Godin's concepts

The great thing about Godin's concepts is that they are relevant to marketers, business people and non-professionals across the board. Succinct and easy to digest, Godin's books offer practical advice backed up with case studies and his own application of the theories, proving that they are accessible to all.

In my professional capacity as CEO of The REaD Group plc, a direct marketing services provider, and chair of the Direct Marketing Association's Data Council I've had the opportunity to watch the direct marketing industry change beyond all recognition in the last 10 years. Indeed, many of the theories that are set out in Godin's book *Permission Marketing*, which once seemed so risqué, now form the backbone of industry best practice and are an accepted way of life for most marketers.

I've certainly followed Godin's work with interest since first encountering him and actually gave copies of *Purple Cow* to my staff to illustrate the shifts taking place in the marketing world. At the time, marketers were fully in the grip of email marketing, old-age media were considered dead and it was all about new, cheap and emerging media channels. However, fast forward to 2011 and Godin's theories have truly come to pass, marketers have spammed the email channel within an inch of its life and they're having to work extra hard to gain attention by marketing remarkable products in remarkable ways across the myriad media channels available.

In Britain companies such as Virgin, John Lewis and online retail brand ASOS which exemplify Godin's theories will more likely survive a challenging retail climate amid global economic turmoil.

The secret to success is about being smart and not insulting the customer's intelligence.

By the same token, our internal marketing department, while satisfying a largely B2B client base, has had to change the way it works. Instead of spending our precious marketing budget on expensive ad campaigns, we're being generous with our ideas and innovative in the way we spread these ideas so that we become thought leaders in our field and give our clients what they want, when they want it and how they want it. We have to practice what we preach.

How it dovetails with other guru theories

Although Godin's theories and the way he delivers them are clearly unique, his hugely influential book *Unleashing the Ideavirus* has very clear parallels with Canadian writer Malcom Gladwell's book *The Tipping Point*. Published in 2000, the books are undoubtedly products of their time.

Both titles deal with the subject of change and they both talk about how ideas and trends spread like viruses, infecting those they come into touch with. They also use similar terminology to describe the people spreading these social viruses. Godin refers to 'sneezers' and Gladwell to 'connectors, mavens and salesmen'.

However, there are subtle yet distinct differences between the texts. Gladwell's book takes a more scientific look at the social epidemics that take place around us, based on the rapid and unexpected environmental change that occurs after a situation has reached critical mass. Godin's standpoint, on the other hand, is grounded in his area of expertise: marketing remarkable ideas in new ways so that they become epidemics in their own right.

Gladwell and Godin certainly seem to hold each other's work in high regard. In fact Gladwell wrote the foreword for *Unleashing the Ideavirus*.

Validity today

Although the last decade has seen unprecedented levels of environmental, social and technological change Godin's theories and concepts have played an intrinsic part in molding and identifying contemporary business trends. Constantly evolving as a writer and thought leader while remaining true to his core beliefs, it would be unwise for anyone to tune out and stop listening to what Godin has to say just yet.

Charles Handy

By Aiz Baig

Name: Charles Handy

Born: 1932

Expertise: Understanding how organizations behave – and to what end; as well as the value of differing structures and approaches to life-learning

Known for: Discontinuous change; portfolio workers; shamrock organization

Best-known titles: *The Age of Unreason* (1989); *Understanding Organizations* (1993); *Gods of Management* (1978); *The Future of Work* (1984); *Inside Organizations* (1990); *The Empty Raincoat* (1994); *The Elephant and the Flea* (2001)

Who is Charles Handy?

Charles Handy graduated from Oriel College, Oxford, with first-class honours in the study of classics, history and philosophy. He has been an oil executive, an economist and a professor at the London Business School. He is acknowledged as one of Europe's best known and most influential management thinkers.

What is Handy known for?

Charles Handy's ground-breaking bestseller *The Age of Unreason* propelled him into the hierarchy of the world's leading management consultants. He further enhanced his reputation as a leading business consultant through his perceptive and comprehensive view of organizations in *Understanding Organizations*.

The concepts

Age of Unreason

The *Age of Unreason* has seven main theories:

1. discontinuous change
2. upside-down thinking
3. shamrock organization
4. triple I organization
5. inverted donut
6. federalism
7. portfolio workers.

Discontinuous change
Non-successive, rapid adjustment, which jeopardizes existing, institutionalized power, because it radically transforms the existing procedures from the manner in which things have been done.

Upside-down thinking
Assumptions that were once held to be fact are being undermined, so a new approach is required. This approach creates new ways of thinking and perceiving familiar things to create innovative solutions.

Shamrock organization
Organization focused on a fundamental team of managers and workers assisted by external full-time and part-time contractors. The first petal symbolizes the fundamental team, the second petal symbolizes external full-time and part-time contractors; 80% of organizational value is conducted by such individuals. The third petal symbolizes the ad hoc labour force. Each petal owes an individualized obligation to the organization. This obligation is based on the wide range of expectation, and contractual arrangements. Each petal requires unique management.

Triple I organization
Organization that focuses on information, intelligence and ideas. This can be formulated into I3=AV, where I3 stands for intelligence, information, ideas and AV stands for added value in cash or kind. There is little differentiation between manager and workers because the emphasis is the pursuit of knowledge. This organization has to be run by consensus. Authority is earned by serving others to enhance their skills, which allows for superior job performance.

Inverted donut

Organization that has a central core of activities and workers surrounded by versatile workers and malleable supply contracts. The core is frequently neglected while the surrounding hole is normally improved in organizations. This can also be applied to personal life.

Federalism

Organization that has decentralized authority. Specific decisions are retained amongst executives; however, the majority of decisions are delegated to middle managers and workers. These organizations are professional and built on high commitment. There is a contractual agreement between both parties.

Portfolio workers

Individuals who balance different careers at different times of their work life to fit in with their personal life to maintain balance. This work is composed of five main categories: wage work (money paid for time given), homework, gift work, study work, fee work (money paid for results delivered).

Understanding Organizations

Handy's second major work was *Understanding Organizations*, which also identified some key theories:

- culture
- motivation
- leadership
- power
- role theory
- working in groups.

Culture

Aggregate of principles and standards adhered to by members of an organization, which guides their relationships with one another and external stakeholders. There are four main cultures: power culture, role culture, task culture and person culture.

> The power culture is where the boss of the organization is at the centre, and is surrounded by widening circles of subordinates. The closer an individual is to the boss, the greater is their influence. This works if the organization is small (< 20 individuals). Such organizations have a quick response to crises because decisions can be made quickly. However, there are two main downsides to such organizations: a high nepotism rate; and if the boss is weak, so too will be the organization.

> The *role culture* is based upon agreed job roles ordered in a logical manner allowing efficient and effective work output with minimal requirement for policy decisions to be made. Workers occupying these roles have well-defined job briefs. Communication is from one job role to another rather than between individuals fulfilling that job role. There is very little change in this organization and it relies on established protocols. There is a high requirement for management rather than leadership in this environment.

> The *task culture* organization is an amalgamation of the power and role cultures. There is a team of individuals with complementary skills able to respond to a variety of projects or tasks. This organization is focused on co-operation among colleagues with little hierarchy. This is possible because these workers are professional competent workers, who require team leaders instead of managers.

The *person culture* is based on the importance of the workers' talent. The workers' special talent accords them status and job security. In this organization, language specific to the special talent is commonplace instead of 'organizational' language. Administration staff have no formal means of 'controlling' these workers.

Motivation

An individual has a combination of needs and of anticipated results. The individual is required to decide the level of effort, energy, excitement, expenditure, etc to invest. In an organizational sense this is governed by the similarity of expectations of the psychological contract between the organization and individual. The greater the overlap between psychological contracts, the greater is the incidence of motivation from both parties.

Leadership

The 'best fit approach' states there is no consistent gold standard of leadership, but that leadership depends upon the leader, subordinates, task and environment. A leader is an individual who forms and communicates a concept that provides guidance to the activities of others. He is faced with four variables that must be taken into consideration: the leader's preference of operating style and personality; the subordinates' preferred choice of leadership, depending on the context; the task, composed of the job, technology and objectives; and the environment, composed of the organizational stance of the leader, the team and significance of the task.

Power

The capability to affect others, resulting in alteration of their perspective and attitude. Organizations are environments in which individuals or groups endeavor to influence others. The distinction between power and influence is that power is the resource and influence is the utilization of that resource. It can only be used if recognized by the individual or group. The potential sources of an individual's power are based on physical power, resource power, position power, expert power and personal power. Physical power is based on superior force (e.g. a tyrant or army commander). Resource power is based on possession of valued resources (e.g. labor force, monetary incentives, promotion, granting of status). Position power is based on an individual's role in the organization (e.g. line manager, CEO).

However, position power depends on the value others place in the individual that occupies that role. Expert power is based on an individual's recognized expertise (e.g. doctor, lawyer, accountant). Personal power (charisma) is based on an individual's personality. It can be enhanced by their position (e.g. Bill Clinton during presidency). Negative power can be any of the previously mentioned powers that may be used illegitimately. This negative power prevents or obstructs actions from occurring (e.g. a civil servant who does not pass messages to superiors). This power normally operates at times of stress, low morale or failure of influence by other means.

Power can be formal, informal or a combination of the two. Formal power is based on resource power (labour force, monetary, promotion, etc). Informal power is based on an individual's knowledge, experience or reputation.

Role theory
A concept to understand the issues and situations of individuals as a unit of organizations. Any individual in any capacity establishes a position with reference to other people. The effectiveness of that capacity will be directly impacted on by themselves (personality, attributes, skills) and the situation's forces. The two

biggest situations for most individuals will be the work group(s) and the family group. This can lead to understanding and increased tolerance for this individual upon understanding the situation. This approach can help identify causes of stress before they become a strain on the individual.

Working in groups
A group is a number of individuals who collectively identify themselves with one another. Organizations utilize groups for problem solving, decision taking, information processing, idea collection, testing/ratifying decisions, coordinating, liaising, increasing commitment/involvement, negotiation/conflict resolution, and inquest/inquiry along with the management, distribution and control of work.

How real companies use Handy's concepts

Discontinuous change can be seen in organizations transforming from a paper-based recording system to electronic. This transformation would no longer require printers, paper, servicing contracts or paper shredders. For Handy's upside-down thinking you must first start with an assumption, such as the National Health Service consultants getting an increase in salary as they get more senior. An alternative would be to pay all consultants the same regardless of seniority, but require less time from more senior consultants. The NHS could employ a greater number of consultants, with younger consultants working harder, but still benefiting from the experience and knowledge of senior consultants.

Continuing with the medical theme, an obvious example of a triple I organization, would be medical school teaching hospitals, where junior doctors come to work, learn and contribute to the improvement of medical conditions. Once this is completed, the individual can either continue to work in a teaching hospital or private practice. Regardless of the work environment, medical professionals are expected to keep abreast of current medical techniques and drugs.

Unilever offers a strong example of Handy's theory of federalism. The company manufactures soap powder in a central European country and distributes Europe-wide, instead of manufacturing it in every European company. The decision on how much soap powder is needed by each country is taken locally.

General Electric has managers of various business units, so follows the shamrock organization structure. Once a new business unit is acquired, external specialists are hired to update the information technology system and provide integration platforms. Once the task has been accomplished they are not longer required until a new business unit is acquired.

A portfolio worker could be a veterinarian who provides locum emergency cover to practices that have veterinarians on holiday for short periods of time. This same emergency veterinarian also helps teach continuing professional development courses at weekends. Lastly, this individual also owns property that is rented to tenants.

How it dovetails with other guru theories

Peter Drucker, who wrote extensively on people management, was a significant influence on Handy's life and work. Additionally, Abraham Maslow, whose hierarchy of needs underpinned much motivation theory, and Edgar Schein, who developed a model of organizational culture in the 1980s, provided works that are closely aligned to Handy's thinking.

Validity today

Charles Handy's theories have influenced managers in every industry throughout the Western world. Entire cohorts of employees have been encouraged to re-evaluate their relationship with organizations concerning greater job flexibility, portfolio careers and ad hoc consultancy. Handy's insights have created a wide range of alternatives to having one career for life, which can be seen on a global scale today.

It will be the exception rather than the rule for an individual to start, work and retire from the same organization. The trend is for individuals to have a portfolio of careers depending on their life stage. Time has only further validated Charles Handy's theories through greater evidence.

Frederick Herzberg

By John Maxted

Name: Frederick Herzberg

Born: 1923; **died:** 2000

Expertise: Clinical psychologist and pioneer of job enrichment

Known for: He is widely regarded as one of the great original thinkers in management and motivational theory

Best-known titles: *The Motivation to Work* (1959); *Work and the Nature of Man* (1966); *The Managerial Choice* (1982); *Herzberg on Motivation* (1983)

Who is Frederick Herzberg?

An American psychologist, Herzberg is famous for introducing job enrichment and the two-factor motivator-hygiene theory. He graduated from City College in 1946 and subsequently held academic posts at the Case Western Reserve University and the University of Utah. He is regarded as the most influential theorist in the field of motivation and his work is as relevant in the 21st century as it was in the 1950s.

What is Herzberg known for?

Herzberg's book *The Motivation to Work*, published in 1959, first established his theories about motivation in the workplace and remains his best-known publication. He continued to develop his motivation-hygiene theory in his subsequent books: *Work and the Nature of Man* (1966); *The Managerial Choice* (1982); and *Herzberg on Motivation* (1983).

As a patrol sergeant in World War II, he was a first-hand witness of the Dachau concentration camp and believed this experience, as well as the talks he had with other Germans living in the area, was what triggered his interest in motivation. Within the field of management science he was certainly influenced by the works of Maslow and his hierarchy of needs theory, and Herzberg has also been a strong influence on many subsequent management science theorists.

Herzberg's research, originally on 200 Pittsburgh engineers and accountants, remains a fundamentally important reference in motivational study. While the study involved a relatively small number of people, Herzberg's considerable preparatory investigations, and the design of the research itself, enabled Herzberg and his colleagues to gather and analyze an extremely sophisticated level of data. His term 'hygiene factors' has now become part of common business parlance.

The concepts

Herzberg's theory of motivation is based on the principle that two factors influence the level of motivation of employees at work. He called these hygiene factors and motivators. These relate to two sets of needs.

1. **Physiological needs:** avoiding unpleasantness or discomfort, and may be fulfilled via money to buy food and shelter etc (hygiene factor).
2. **Psychological needs:** the need for personal development fulfilled by activities which cause one to grow (motivator). He reasoned that because the factors causing satisfaction are different from those causing dissatisfaction, the two feelings cannot be treated as opposites of one another. The opposite of satisfaction is not dissatisfaction but rather no satisfaction. Similarly, the opposite of dissatisfaction is no dissatisfaction.

Hygiene factors

A hygiene factor is something which is required for an employee not to become dissatisfied, but its presence does not mean that an employee will be motivated. Examples of hygiene factors include company policy, quality of supervision, relationship with boss, working environment and conditions, salary, relationship with peers and sense of security. These factors do not motivate people and do not in themselves provide employees with intrinsic work satisfaction. These factors are what Herzberg calls *movers* i.e. factors which move employees to perform tasks but do not motivate them to add value and deliver high performance. Herzberg's work established that money in itself is not a motivator but a mover, in that people are incentivized to work for money because of what it can buy them, not from the intrinsic value of the money.

Herzberg sometimes refers to hygiene factors as KITA (kick in the arse) factors, which is the process of providing incentives or threat of punishment to cause someone to do something. He argues that these provide only a short-run success because the motivator factors that determine whether there is satisfaction or no satisfaction are intrinsic to the job itself, and do not result from carrot-and-stick incentives.

Motivators

These are factors which enrich the content of the actual work which employees are asked to do. They provide opportunities to learn, develop and improve an employee's quality of working life. Examples of motivators include sense of achievement, autonomy, recognition, responsibility, personal growth and advancement. Herzberg argued that if managers give employees the opportunity to grow and fulfill themselves as human beings, then they will be motivated to excel and add value rather than just be moved to perform tasks.

He uses the term *job enrichment* to describe what is required for intrinsic motivation and this has become a cornerstone in job design and management training. The purpose of job enrichment is to improve the quality of an employee's job and therefore motivate the employee to accomplish more. Herzberg defines job enrichment as a continuous management process with the outcome of turning employees' effort into performance. To achieve this, the overall corporate mission statement should be communicated to all and each employee should know exactly how he or she fits into the overall process.

Employees need to be provided with the right resources and support functions, such as information technology, communication technology and personnel training and development. Creating a supportive and blame-free corporate culture, removing elements that foster mistrust and politicking and providing a free flow of information are all key hygiene factors.

True job enrichment involves providing employees with the opportunity to develop in their roles and Herzberg argues that no-one should be required to perform a task which they are overqualified for. Roles should be designed where there is variety, scope for personal influence over how the task is performed and an intrinsic understanding and recognition of and feedback on how an employee's efforts are contributing to the overall success of an organization. Herzberg also introduced the term *job enlargement*, which refers to the need to design a job which allows an employee to undertake a broader range of tasks, which can make the role more relevant and significant.

Equally important is the need to link employees' performance directly to reward and to understand what reward employees want, and not always assume that everyone wants the same thing. Herzberg's view was that both factors are equally important, but that good hygiene will only lead to average performance, preventing dissatisfaction but not, by itself, creating a positive attitude or motivation to work. To motivate the employee, management must enrich the content of the actual work it asks them to do. For example, this may involve building into tasks a greater level of responsibility and providing the opportunity to learn new skills. And by advocating making work more interesting the quality of the work experience is improved for the individual.

In summary, the main conclusions that Herzberg reached in his research are as follows.

- People are made dissatisfied by a bad environment, but they are seldom made satisfied by a good environment.
- The prevention of dissatisfaction is just as important as encouragement of motivator satisfaction.
- Hygiene factors operate independently of motivation factors. An individual can be highly motivated in his work and be dissatisfied with his work environment.
- All hygiene factors are equally important, although their frequency of occurrence differs considerably.
- Hygiene improvements have short-term effects. Any improvements result in a short-term removal of, or prevention of, dissatisfaction.
- Hygiene needs are cyclical in nature and come back to a starting point. This leads to the 'what have you done for me lately?' syndrome.
- Hygiene needs have an escalating zero point and no final answer.

How real companies use Herzberg's concepts

One of the great and enduring features of Herzberg's contribution to management science is its wide application across commerce and industry. Most organizations now conduct employee satisfaction studies to understand what really motivates their staff. Work is structured in a way where employees see the opportunity to develop within a role. Jobs are enlarged to give employees the satisfaction of seeing more purpose from their output. Organizations have become expert at communicating the mission and purpose of the business to staff so that they feel significant and relevant to the company's success. Feedback on performance is now commonplace, both through formal appraisals as well as ongoing support and coaching. Employers have realized the importance of recognizing achievement in their staff and many have introduced award schemes such as naming an 'employee of the month'. Research has shown that employees find this type of award more motivating than a cash bonus, especially if peers and customers have voted for them. Many organizations now have incorporated job rotation into working practices, which not only provides employees with greater variety but also gives employers a significantly more flexible workforce. Research has shown that manufacturing companies that place the name of an employee somewhere on a product who either made or certified its quality enjoy much higher levels of customer satisfaction. This is because the employee feels a personal responsibility for the product and a pride in ensuring its quality. One example of this is a mail-order organic and eco-friendly gardening company in Cornwall called Rocket Gardens. It sends plants to the customer's door and always names the person responsible, ensuring that the customer in receipt is in no doubt of the personal touch involved.

There is no shortage of examples of how companies have applied Herzberg's concepts to achieve corporate success. In the 1980s Sir Colin Marshall turned round the fortunes of British Airways to create the 'world's favorite airline' in just a few years. A key part of this success was achieved through a program called 'putting people first'. This was a major change program to empower customer service staff to take more personal responsibility for the delivery of service excellence and was underpinned by Herzberg's principles. The airline put in place schemes to recognize and reward high levels of service, increased the scope for local decision making and ran a program of two-day courses attended by all customer-facing staff where employees had the mission of the business and their roles in achieving explained to them in detail. They were also encouraged to suggest new initiatives which could contribute to the company achieving its goal of building the world's favorite airline. As a result people felt empowered, engaged and personally responsible for the airline's success.

More recently, the leading retailer Tesco recognized how motivated staff who are committed to their work have a positive effect on company performance. The company invests several million pounds each year in training programs which are based on Herzberg motivators. These have resulted in the following.

- New and more open lines of communication between managers and staff.
- Directors and senior managers spending a week on the shop floor listening to ideas from customers and staff.
- A scheme to spot individual talent and to fast-track shop floor workers up the promotional ladder.
- A better understanding of individual employees' personal circumstances.

These initiatives have helped Tesco deliver record growth and sales profits and illustrate how effectively Herzberg's theory may be used in practice.

How it dovetails with other guru theories

It is generally accepted that the founding father of modern theory of motivation was Abraham Maslow, who published *Motivation and Personality* in 1954, and he certainly influenced Herzberg's work. Maslow's theory assumes that motivation is based on the satisfaction of basic needs and subsequent motivation theorists all agree that people are concerned with fulfilling needs, whether emotional, intellectual or spiritual. Most modern theories are collectively called 'content' theories of motivation.

Herzberg's work has influenced many subsequent management gurus, including Douglas McGregor, David McClelland and Clayton Alderferer to name but three, and indeed his work continues to be the foundation for much of the contemporary research into motivation and employee engagement.

McGregor is most well-known for his Theory X and Y concepts of motivation and approaches to management. The link between these and Herzberg's hygiene factors and motivators is clear. In Theory X employees are seen to be work shy and untrustworthy. They work because they have to and require close supervision and implicit and explicit threats in order for them to perform. In contrast, Theory Y assumes that employees are eager to fulfill their potential to develop and express their innate creativity. No one goes to work to do a bad job and managers need to enable and empower employees to get the best results.

David McClelland identified three types of needs which dominate the behavior of individuals: achievement, power and affiliation. Most people experience combined needs for the three, though certain people demonstrate a marked preference for a particular need above the other two.

Validity today

There is no doubt that Herzberg's work is as relevant now as it was 50 years ago. Indeed with the much-documented research around generation Y, there is a need for employers to provide work which is even more meaningful for a generation of young people whose expectations of personal fulfillment have never been higher. In the early 21st century we now see a generation of new 'gazelle' organizations such as Microsoft, Apple, Google and Virgin which have become global players and have quickly achieved incredible success. Much of this success has come from quickly realizing the potential of a large number of highly able employees, fundamentally through applying Herzberg's principles of empowering and engagement.

With the significant advances in technology, much of the mundane and routine work which existed 50 years ago has now been automated, and with a more highly educated workforce there is now more opportunity to create jobs which allow more people to grow in their careers and fulfill their potential. Herzberg's influence in developments associated with work design and methods of management to provide job satisfaction and motivation may therefore now be even more important.

Napoleon Hill

By Andrew Scott

Name: Napoleon Hill

Born: 1883; **died:** 1970

Expertise: Author, journalist, lawyer and lecturer on self-empowerment and success, Napoleon Hill was also an active entrepreneur, magazine publisher and adviser to President Roosevelt

Known for: 'What the mind of man can conceive and believe, it can achieve'

Best-known titles: *The Law of Success* (1928); *Think and Grow Rich* (1937); *Napoleon Hill's Keys to Success: The 17 Principles of Personal Achievement; Success Through a Positive Mental Attitude* (1960)

Who is Napoleon Hill?

Napoleon Hill is arguably the great grandfather of all modern business and self-help books. In 1908, the steel magnate Andrew Carnegie challenged a young Napoleon Hill to compile a 'philosophy for successes'. He introduced Hill to his prominent peers for interviews (amongst others Henry Ford) but extended no payment, citing the opportunity as reward enough.

Hill had already experienced some business success running a mine and working in sales at a lumber yard, before losing it all in the stock market crash of 1907. A tenacious young man, he recognized the value of the opportunity immediately and began a challenging personal journey, supporting his family while seeking to achieve his goal.

Most of Hill's life was dedicated to discovering the human qualities which enable one person to achieve success where another might fail. Despite significant setbacks, he pursued his goal in an exhaustive manner until he found the answers. He published numerous works, each communicating this revolutionary philosophy for success with ever greater clarity.

What is Hill known for?

The Law of Success was published in 1928, weighing in at a hefty 1,500 pages in eight volumes. For the next decade Hill lectured, ran a business magazine, lost all his wealth (again) got divorced and worked for President Roosevelt as an adviser and speech writer.

In 1937 Hill released (after the late addition of a chapter called 'The Mystery of Sexual Transmutation') a new, streamlined version of *The Law of Success*. *Think and Grow Rich: Teaching, for the first time, the famous Andrew Carnegie formula for money-making, based upon the thirteen proven steps to riches* (its original full title) was an instant success, selling out the initial 5,000 print run in under three weeks.

Think and Grow Rich is probably the most well-researched book in history on the origins of success. It is based on the analysis of 500 interviews with America's most successful people and was 25 years in the making.

Hill published a further eight books, alongside some audio and film recordings.

The concepts

The core message of Hill's work is that putting his 13 principles of success into action toward a definiteness of purpose, in concert with genuine belief in your ability to achieve it, will enable you to be successful in life. These principles are supported by anecdotes explaining the root of the principles and demonstrating them in action with real-world examples.

The 13 principles are as follows.

1. **Desire**. You have to have a real desire for success, in order to achieve it. Hill explains that this is the only starting point from which your road to riches – monetary or otherwise – can be built. 'Wishing' for something is not enough, it must be a true desire which becomes an obsession, which is combined with

planning of definite ways and means to acquire riches and backed by a persistence which does not recognize failure.

In the remaining 12 steps, Hill explains how your desire is then used to fuel the practical process of achieving your goals.

2. **Faith.** Hill argues this can only be achieved by the practical application of all 13 principles, because it is a state of mind which develops voluntarily. All you can do is feed your subconscious the right ingredients through affirmative actions. Faith is induced by auto-suggestion, through repetition of thought. If you lack self-confidence to apply this he provides a practical formula to achieve it based on a daily repetition of your definiteness of purpose, concentration on your future self while eradicating negative thought or action toward others, because such negativity in others will never bring success to you.

3. **Auto-suggestion.** Also described as self-suggestion, this is the repeating of your desire to yourself every morning and evening, in order to program it into your subconscious mind.

4. **Specialized knowledge.** Specific knowledge harvested from any sources in order to achieve your purpose. Hill argues that it is not the specialist knowledge which is hard to find, but that the skill is in translating that knowledge into practical plans to achieve success. To do that you require imagination.

5. **Imagination.** This is described as coming in two forms: (a) synthetic imagination – this fashions old or existing concepts, knowledge and ideas into new combinations; (b) creative imagination – this is where hunches and inspirations come from. Hill says we must give life and action to ideas, which then harbor power of their own and live beyond our physical form when we die.

6. **Organized planning.** A clear and concise plan to turn your desire into positive action. In one of the most involved

chapters, Hill diverges deeply into the building blocks to make it happen. The advice ranges from creating your 'mastermind alliance' (a group of people to have around you who are smart, positive, supportive and successful), the sectors of society where new leadership will be required in future, how to get a job, how to write a brief, marketing, the QQS rating of your service (quality, quantity and spirit) and 30 major causes of failure. Organized planning is treated as a pseudonym for leadership. Hill lists major attributes of successful leadership, and identifies causes of leadership failure.

7. **Decision.** In a study of 25,000 men and women who had experienced failure, Hill says indecision was at the top of the 30 causes of failure. Hill argues that the art of making a decision is so critical to life that it should be taught in schools or colleges. He says decision almost always requires courage. Without definiteness of decision, your plans, however good, cannot be actioned.

8. **Persistence.** You must persist without exception. Hill rates persistence second only to desire in importance to achieve your definite major purpose. This is because desire directly impacts the strength of your resolve: your persistence. If you ever feel yourself losing your persistence, he argues, you need to light a greater fire under your desire. Persistence is a state of mind, thus we have control over it and must feed it appropriately with a desire allied with a definite major purpose.

9. **Power of the mastermind.** You will never know everything and so you should find a group of positive, successful people whom you can spend time with to help spark new ideas and reinforce your resolve. By spending time with them some of their success and positive mental attitude will rub off on you.

10. **The mystery of sex transmutation.** Sex is the strongest of all human desires. Transmutation is the ability to channel the energy of this desire for sex into other, productive activities.

11. **The subconscious mind.** You cannot control your subconscious mind, but only feed it with a larger amount of positive rather than negative thoughts and experiences (auto-suggestion or self-suggestion). The conscious mind consumes everything you experience and therefore you have to make a conscious choice to be positive. The subconscious mind can only render back what you put in to it and you have no control over that process, other than to contribute in a positive way to what it is fed through active positive thought and seeking environments and people who provide positive experiences.

12. **The brain.** In the human brain the 'creative-imagination' is the receiving station of the mind and the 'subconscious mind' the sender. By actively engaging in all 13 principles, you will be communicating with the universal intelligence of the ether.

13. **The sixth sense.** The conduit between the mind and infinite intelligence; it is a combination of the spiritual and physical. Hill argues that only through practising all 12 other principles – and over a prolonged period – will you be able to really appreciate and experience fully the power of your sixth sense, as many great leaders have done in the past.

How real companies use Hill's concepts

Many great leaders across the spectrum of success, from senior politicians to business chiefs, can be identified as having applied one or a few of Hill's 13 principles to great effect. A burning desire to succeed is usually a prerequisite for any successful person, but very few leaders or organizations have been consistent in applying all of Hill's 'major attributes of successful leadership'.

Margaret Thatcher was a proponent of 'Any decision is better than no decision', but certainly failed on the cooperation front. Eventually, this failing cost her the office of Prime Minister.

Richard Branson and his Virgin empire is largely perceived as a do-gooding under-dog, thanks largely to Branson's own cultivation of that image. Virgin does have many projects which impact on the world positively and their customer service is better than many – but Richard's own extravagant self-promotion has at times alienated both customers and even his employees.

The Nordstrom chain of stores (started in 1901, before Hill started his masterwork) has even today a reputation for 'going the extra mile', a cornerstone of Hill's works. The decision to 'go the extra mile' for a customer, friend or colleague encompasses many of the facets outlined in the 13 principles.

Business has attempted to embrace some of the principles Hill promotes but few, if any at all, have actively and consistently deployed them all.

As modern consumers become further educated and globalization continues to extend the privilege of choice across ever wider markets in the new knowledge economy, business and its leadership will be forced, out of economic necessity, to embrace many of Hill's principles – including those more esoteric practices – not only to better perform operationally but to be the acceptable or preferred choice of their customer base.

How it dovetails with other guru theories

The '13 principles of success' have been much imitated. Hill's core philosophy that only through real and consistent belief can we achieve our goals is now an accepted part of the science of achievement. In seeking to communicate the recipe for success, Hill disregarded luck, and instead promoted a 'definiteness of purpose' in life.

This is very much in line with the bulk of self-help works on the market today – taking control of your own destiny through self-determination. *The 7 Habits of Highly Effective People* by Stephen Covey (over 15 million copies sold worldwide) owes much to Hill's work and approach.

From 1952 to 1962, Hill lectured on his philosophy of personal achievement. The 'Science of Success' course was given in association with W Clement Stone, and in 1960 Hill and Stone co-authored the book *Success Through a Positive Mental Attitude*. As of 2011, six of the 10 bestselling books on Amazon about positive mental thinking are versions of Hill or Stone's work.

In 2009 Barbara Ehrenreich published *Bright-Sided: How the Relentless Promotion of Positive Thinking Has Undermined America* as a reaction to a plethora of positive-thinking books, such as the *The Secret*, published in 2009 by Rhonda Byrne.

The work of writer William Walker Atkinson (a pioneer of the US 'new thought' movement, which promoted the power of the mind and the concept of God as ubiquitous 'infinite intelligence') shares similarities with the parts of Hill's work which discuss facets of the spiritual, but the bulk of his advice is rooted in changing one's own habits and developing a self-discipline to action.

Validity today

Hill's legacy is hard to overestimate. In one form or another *Think and Grow Rich* has been in print ever since it was published in 1937 (excluding the paper rationing period of World War II).

Today, the work has been re-published in hundreds of languages, abridged and repackaged. It remains highly respected, and although many of the supporting anecdotes in the book reference companies and people long dead, they support the theories adequately. In some reworked versions of the text these older examples have been replaced with more up-to-date studies.

Think and Grow Rich remains the bestselling of Hill's books. *Business Week* magazine ranked *Think and Grow Rich* as the sixth bestselling paperback business book, 70 years after it was first published!

Hill taught that the strength of your conviction that you will reach your goal is directly proportionate to your physical world ability to attract the people and situations which will lend help to your cause. For the first time he boldly and precisely articulated to a mass audience the connection between the practical actions needed to make money or create success, and the spiritual beliefs and psychological conditioning of the individual.

The longevity of his work pays tribute to a lifetime of interviews and research, as a writer who genuinely tried to practice what he preached and often succeeded.

Guy Kawasaki

By Andrew Scott

Name: Guy Kawasaki

Born: 1954

Expertise: Technology evangelism, internet business, ethics and start-ups

Known for: Being a business guru for the internet generation, his ethos of ethical and decent conduct in business and 'the art of being a mensch'

Best-known titles: *The Art of the Start* (2004); *Rules for Revolutionaries* (2000); *The Macintosh Way* (1990)

Who is Guy Kawasaki?

Guy Kawasaki worked at Apple Computer Inc in the early 1980s, eventually becoming chief evangelist. He describes owing his old Stanford University roommate Mike Boich a 'great debt' for getting him a job there.

He has subsequently built a reputation for cultivating a progressive way of doing business, much of which grew from his experience championing the Macintosh computer. It was at Apple that the seeds of his 'secular evangelism' began to germinate.

He remains a bright light in the technology sector, but in recent years has crossed over to the mainstream, evangelizing to a wider audience a highly customer-centric approach to product and service delivery, allied to a strong moral compass, via his books, public speaking and in his consultancy roles.

In 2011 Kawasaki co-founded Alltop (a website which aggregates popular topics on the web) and was founding partner of Silicon Valley investment firm Garage Technology Ventures.

What is Kawasaki known for?

Although he has started at least three technology companies since leaving Apple in 1987, it is for being an author, prolific blogger, speaker and technology investor that Kawasaki has become best known.

Guy's most widely recognized book is probably *The Art of The Start*. Published in 2004 and quickly embraced by internet technology companies (as a bible on 'bootstrapping' a company from an idea through to investment), the advice is not specific to the technology sector. It is as much an indirect manifesto on human interaction as it is a how-to guide for the uninitiated who might be looking to start a business, or someone trying to innovate at an existing company.

A vocal proponent of 'focusing on the customer', Kawasaki also introduced 'the art of being a mensch' to the collective consciousness of a generation of entrepreneurs. 'Mensch' is a Yiddish term used to describe someone who acts ethically, is decent and admirable.

These are the two core themes which Guy has returned to throughout his writing career: of a morally defensible approach to doing business and a laser-like focus on what your customers want.

The concepts

The Macintosh Way focused on the promotion and marketing of technology products. It includes many anecdotes from his time at Apple, evangelizing the then revolutionary Macintosh computer. Kawasaki further relays the lessons from these heady days in *How To Drive Your Competition Crazy*, explaining what to do and what not to do to gain a differential advantage, particularly as an underdog in the marketplace. He then built on these experiences to form what the author himself described as 'a weapon of mass construction' with *The Art of the Start*, a remarkably accessible dissertation on getting an idea off the ground.

Shunning many traditional management habits, two key principles (creation of meaning and menschood) stand out as over-arching values with which to run your business. These two principles sandwich many smaller practical concepts.

Create meaning

If one word had to be used to describe the book, it would be evangelization. The gospel being evangelized in this case is described by Kawasaki as a mantra for your business.

The right mantra will help to prioritize the customer, focusing on what is important for your business and discarding what is not. Kawasaki promotes the idea that you need to understand and embrace what 'meaning' you are trying to create as a business, from which everything else can follow.

Ideally, this should be articulated as a three-word mantra, representing a meaning which can be communicated to your employees and embraced as a core part of the business culture.

Kawasaki gives examples throughout of traditional thinking versus his approach. The Red Cross, for example, whose mission statement reads 'To help people prevent, prepare for and respond to emergencies', he hypothesizes would be better served with the mantra 'Stop suffering'.

He argues that to create meaning in a business by evangelizing a mantra, rather than a mission statement, is more effective, evoking power and emotion in your disciples – exactly what you need to be a successful entrepreneur. A mantra stands in contrast to a dry mission statement, which often describes an operational activity using overused weightless words such as 'best', 'quality' and 'leader' to describe a business.

The book is full of practical advice which can be applied at each step while starting whatever it is you want to start, such as the following.

- **Choose a good name.** Begin with a letter early in the alphabet, choose something which has potential to be used as a verb, avoid the trendy and make sure it 'sounds' appropriate to what you do.
- **Position** your business as opposite to your competition, avoiding overly used words which carry no differentiation. Make it personal, e.g. instead of 'Reduces the size of the ozone hole' you would say 'Prevents you from getting melanoma'.
- **Presentations should follow the 10-20-30 rule:** 10 slides for a 20 minute pitch using 30 point text (meaning you can't over-fill the slide with content).
- When raising investment, **write an** executive summary in plain English (maximum four paragraphs) and use it to spark interest. Don't use it to try to deliver every detail of your business plan.
- Kawasaki promotes an **agile approach to product or service development**. Forget investing months in research, instead get something out there in the wild as fast as possible.
- Especially when starting a new venture, '**niche thyself**'. Strive to be unique and provide value to your customer. Focus on doing one thing really well first; this simplifies everything.
- On **recruiting** Kawasaki says **trust your gut with people** and be disciplined about following up references *before* an interview. Note the dangers of hiring from a corporate world, where someone may not be used to getting his or her hands dirty. You should always try to hire someone better than yourself.

- To aid your operational roadmap weave a 'MAT' or set of **milestones, assumptions and tasks**. The milestones are not sector specific:

  - prove your concept
  - complete design specifications
  - finish a prototype
  - raise capital
  - ship a testable version to customers
  - ship the final version to customers
  - achieve break even.

- Then **list every significant assumption** relating to your organization, from gross margin to sales cycle length to the cost of your bill of materials and team remuneration. Continually measure and amend these, as real-world experience proves them right or wrong.
- Your **list of tasks** should be those things which, although not critical, are still required to achieve your milestones; such as renting office space, getting insurances etc.
- Then Kawasaki comes full circle back to **evangelization: seed the clouds to make it rain**. Let 'a hundred flowers blossom' by enabling test drives of your product or service for free, thus lowering the barriers to entry.
- You must seek out the influencers and embrace them – if B2B they may not always be where you expect in the hierarchy of a target organization.

Menschood

The final chapter asks us to behave throughout our business dealings with good will and embrace 'the art of being a mensch', a Yiddish word which in practical terms means you should:

- help many people
- do what is right
- pay back society.

All the advice in his book has passed through these three filters. For any entrepreneur it represents a reminder of what should be important when running a business.

As examples, he cites observing the spirit of agreements, not just the letter (e.g. a commission payment not due because an agreement lapsed seven days before it should be paid anyway), paying for what you get (e.g. a supplier undercharging you should be reported) and focusing on what is important (e.g. this may not always be simply to win at all costs).

He argues that your company and each employee in your company operate in the wider context of society. Kawasaki is not promoting being soft in business, rather, that doing things which are bad for society does not scale. That ultimately, it will not generate longevity of shareholder value.

How real companies use Kawasaki's concepts

Start-ups

AirBnB is a website which enables people to rent space in their homes to others. It started after the founders, Brian Chesky and Joe Gebbia, stumbled upon the idea after visiting San Francisco in 2007 and wanting somewhere affordable to stay. They stayed on someone's floor on an air mattress. AirBnB was born.

They had a tough, bootstrapping first year and survived by embracing guerilla tactics. This created some buzz, but not the flood of customers they needed. At one point, the founders had literally lived their own customer experience for months, moving from place to place – using their own site to find living accommodation. You can't get much closer to your customers than that.

Although not yet hitting hockey-stick growth, the determination and innovation of the pair did persuade the founder of the business incubator program 'Y Combinator' to enroll them on his course. In 2010 AirBnB raised $7.2m in funding from two Silicon Valley venture capital firms on top of its earlier seed funding of $600,000. Today the founders maintain that the lack of money helped to define a culture of frugality and forced them to focus on what the customer wanted.

Both founders regularly speak at events attended by hundreds of entrepreneurs, a sign that the success has not gone to their heads. Their self-deprecating presentation demonstrates a desire to give back to the ecosystem and have others learn from their mistakes – a big step toward Kawasaki's menschood.

Corporates

Apple remains one of the champions of delivering a user-centric product experience. Its revolutionary iPod and iPhones have become the trend setters in their markets. This ability to deliver something which is very customer focused in its design remains the primary reason for Apple's success and continues an approach which crystalized while Kawasaki was still at Apple.

Bricks and mortar

At Pret A Manger, a UK sandwich and coffee chain, even senior staff have to work at the tills before they take up their managerial roles, and customer service is evangelized as a priority to all employees. Staff are empowered to make decisions which enable them to serve customers well.

How it dovetails with other guru theories

Maverick! The Success Story Behind the World's Most Unusual Workplace by Ricardo Semler is possibly the ultimate reference work on running your company with an empowered workforce. To effect change in an organization so fundamentally that staff can chose their own salary levels needs more than a policy change, it needs an evangelized mantra.

Rework by Jason Fried takes a similarly untraditional approach, providing an even more quickfire set of start-up tips and philosophical statements on building your business.

Kawasaki himself has continued to evolve his evangelization theme into his latest work, *Enchantment: The Art of Changing Hearts, Minds, and Actions*. In it, he builds on his two original core principles and explains how to influence what people will do while maintaining the highest standards of ethics.

Validity today

A lecturer at Santa Barbara's Technology Management Faculty says he has given out *The Art of the Start* to his New Venture Creation class for the past five years. 'Quarter after quarter', he says 'it has inspired and enlightened my students.'

Anecdotal evidence in 2011 would suggest that *The Art of the Start* remains both relevant and timely. Today, the ability of any web-related company to iterate its product or service at speed (i.e. testing and optimizing its offering live in the marketplace) is reshaping traditional business thinking on how you take a product to market, the incumbents you are able to challenge and the size of the associated funding required to do so. This customer-focused approach, led by market testing, is the very gospel preached in *The Art of the Start*.

The barriers to starting a business in any sector continue to fall. *The Art of the Start* captures the essence of a new philosophy of bootstrapping, rapid development and launch: build it, try and get it out to customers and iterate on their feedback.

Arguably, 'the art of being a mensch' has not been as universally embraced as much of Kawasaki's more practical business advice. But there are exceptions. At one end of the scale, 'ICE' is a group of entrepreneurs who commit to helping one another on the basis of trust and not for profit. At the opposite end, Bill Gates has established the Bill and Melinda Gates Foundation with an endowment in excess of $40bn, literally changing the world for the better. Leadership must come from the top. Who better to be led by than a mensch with a mantra?

Richard Koch

By Colin Barrow

Name: Richard Koch

Born: 1950

Expertise: A management consulting authority, who has also made a series of successful investments in businesses where the 80/20 rule was applied

Known for: His books on how to apply the 80/20 rule, otherwise known as the Pareto principle, in and outside of business and organizational life

Best-known titles: *The 80/20 Principle* (1997); *The Power Laws* (2000), published in the US as *The Natural Laws of Business* (2001); *The 80/20 Revolution* (2002), published in the US as *The 80/20 Individual* (2003); *Living the 80/20 Way* (2004); *Superconnect: The power of networks and the strength of weak links* (2010), co-authored with Greg Lockwood

Who is Richard Koch?

Koch is an Oxford graduate with an MBA from Wharton (University of Pennsylvania). He worked in the Boston Consulting Group and Bain and Company before starting his own management consulting firm, LEK Consulting, with Jim Lawrence and Iain Evans. Through investments in Betfair, Filofax, the Great Little Trading Company and Plymouth Gin, Koch has put the 80/20 concept to good use in making a personal fortune.

What is Koch known for?

Originally commissioned to write a book on business strategy, Koch showed his early draft, including a half page on the 80/20 principle (that 80% of results come from 20% of effort), to a publisher friend. They suggested devoting a whole book to the principle. Despite some initial reservations Koch eventually produced *The 80/20 Principle*, published in 1997. With close on a million sales the book has become a world bestseller. Japan and Korea account for nearly a quarter of those sales. Translated into 33 languages and 14 years after the first edition, a new edition is still selling well.

Koch has extended the application of the 80/20 principle into aspects of everyday life, so reaching markets outside the reach of general business books.

> If you're not enjoying something, or feeling that it is really important and useful, stop doing it. You have to stop doing things to discover what is truly important.

This quote summarizes Koch's central idea on how everyone can use his approach in every area of their lives.

As with many gurus, Koch's genius lies not in inventing or discovering a concept, but in turning an established truth into a practical tool that anyone can use. The idea that people spend much of their time and energy on tasks of little or no importance is not exactly new. This quotation attributed to a Roman soldier a century or so BC confirms the suspicion that time wasting is a well-established organizational fact.

> We trained hard, but it seemed that every time
> we were beginning to form up into teams, we
> would be reorganized. I was to learn later in
> life that we tend to meet any new situation by
> reorganization; and what a wonderful method it can
> be for creating the illusion of progress while producing
> confusion, inefficiency and demoralization.

The concepts

Vilfredo Pareto (1848–1923) was the originator of Koch's 80/20 formula. Pareto studied classics and then engineering at the Polytechnic Institute of Turin. His first job was as a director of the Rome Railway Company, after which he became managing director of an iron and steel concern, the Società Ferriere d'Italia in Florence. He reinvented himself as an economist and his research led him to note that the unequal distribution of wealth in his country followed a recognizable pattern. Twenty percent of the people owned 80% of the wealth.

Koch's work is a re-interpretation of Pareto as applied to every aspect of life and not just to business or economics. Seven steps underpin Koch's approach to what he defines as a time revolution rather than 'another time management system'.

1. **Make the difficult mental leap of dissociating effort from reward.** Getting away from the idea that hard work, rooted deep in the psychology of the Protestant work ethic, is its own reward. Citing Warren Buffett, who makes it a virtue to hold only a handful of companies' shares and to hold onto them, compared to the typical fund-management approach which he has dubbed 'the Noah's Ark method', he says, 'One buys two of everything and ends up with a zoo.'

2. **Give up guilt and spend your time only doing things you enjoy**, as, according to Koch, there's no value in doing things that you don't enjoy. Most rich or successful people enjoy and have been passionate about what they do – Branson, Sugar, Attenborough – another indication of the universe's 80/20 perversity. Some 20% of people have both 80% of wealth and 80% of the enjoyment to be had from work. That leaves 80% of people doing dull work for little reward – a proposition that certainly strikes a chord.

3. **Free yourself up from being controlled by others** – 'it's a fair bet that when 80% of time yields 20% of results, that 80% is being undertaken at the behest of other people'. Koch goes on to state that the best way to get round this problem is to act as if you owned the organization even if you don't. That doesn't mean neglecting obligations and responsibilities, rather taking full ownership and so getting more satisfaction and correspondingly better results.

4. **'Be unconventional and even eccentric in your use of time.'** Question whether attending meetings, filling in forms and all the routines of conventional organizational life are really essential. Koch claims that in order to avoid the likelihood

that 80% of your time will be spent on low-priority activities you should adopt unconventional behavior or solutions deviating as far from the norm as you can 'without being thrown out of your world'.

5. **List the 20% of activities that produce 80% of the results you want to achieve**. Then make another list of the activities that give you 80% of happiness or personal satisfaction.

6. **Build 'happiness islands' and 'achievement islands'**. This is done by identifying the elements common to both the step four lists and concentrating your time on them.

7. The last of Koch's seven routes to time revolution is '**to eliminate or reduce the low-value activities**. For the 80% of activities that give you only 20% of results, the ideal is to eliminate them. You may need to do this anyway before you can allocate more time to the high-value activities.'

Koch's parting shot is his top 10 list of low-value uses of time.

> First of all, things other people want you to do. Second, things that have always been done this way. Third, things that you are not unusually good at doing. Fourth, things you don't enjoy doing. Number five, things that are always interrupted. Sixth, things that few other people are interested in. Seventh, the things that have already taken twice as long as you originally expected. Eighth, things for which your collaborators are unreliable or low quality. Ninth, things that have a predictable cycle. And my number 10 low-value use of time is answering the telephone.

How real companies use Koch's concepts

Look at the table below, which is a real example showing the number of customers a salesperson had, the value of their sales and the value of their potential sales. This more or less confirms the rule, as 18% of customers account for 78% of sales.

The misallocated sales cost

Number of customers		Value of actual sales		Value of sales potential 2 years out	
	%	£'000	%	£'000	%
4	3	710	69	1,200	71
21	18	800	78	1,500	88
47	41	918	90	1,600	94
116	100	1,025	100	1,700	100

Interestingly enough, when the salesperson in the company used in the above example was asked where he thought his sales in two years' time would be coming from (see last column in the table), he felt that his top 18% of customers would account for 88% of sales (up from 78% of actual sales this year).

An analysis of this salesperson's call reports showed that over 60% of time was spent calling on the bottom 68 accounts, and they planned to continue doing so. As these customers accounted for little more than 10% of sales, time was being seriously misallocated. As the salesperson expected the top 25 accounts would account for most of the future growth this misallocation of resource was scheduled to get worse. This 'activity', rather than a results-based outlook, was being used by the sales manager to make out a case for an additional salesperson. What was actually needed was a call grading system to lower the call rate on accounts with the least sales potential. So, for example, accounts with the least potential were called on twice a year and phoned twice, whilst top-grade accounts were visited up to eight times a year. When introduced, the grading process saved costs, eliminated the need for an additional salesperson and freed up time so the salesman could prospect for new, high-potential accounts.

How it dovetails with other guru theories

Koch's theory is that the 80/20 rule applies across every aspect of life. Pareto himself was more cautious in his claims for the relationship, saying only the following:

> This law being empirical, it may not always remain true, especially not for all mankind. At present, however, the statistics which we have present no exceptions to the law; it may therefore provisionally be accepted as universal. But exceptions may be found, and I should not be greatly surprised if some day a well-authenticated exception was discovered.

Others recognized the same relationship in their own areas of expertise, including quality and cost management pioneer – Dr Joseph Juran (1904–2008). In the late 1940s, as a result of his courses at New York University and seminars at the American Management Association, he had come to recognize the principle of the 'vital few and trivial many' as a true 'universal', applicable not only in numerous managerial functions but in the physical and biological worlds generally. Whilst writing the first edition of *Quality Control Handbook*, Durnan commented:

> I was faced squarely with the need for giving a short name to the universal. In the resulting write-up under the heading 'Maldistribution of Quality Losses', I listed numerous instances of such maldistribution as a basis for generalization. I also noted that Pareto had found wealth to be maldistributed. In addition, I showed examples of the now familiar cumulative curves, one for maldistribution of wealth and the other for maldistribution of quality losses.

Since Juran adopted the idea, it might better be called 'Juran's assumption'. That assumption is that most of the results in any situation are determined by a small number of causes.

Pareto after Juran

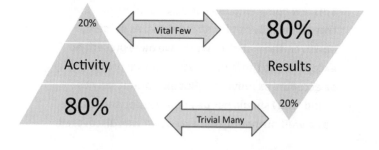

Others, including Cyril Northcote Parkinson, noted maldistribution in spheres outside of wealth. Parkinson's Law, as it became known, states that 'work expands so as to fill the time available for its completion'. This was the first sentence of a humorous essay published in *The Economist* in 1955, later expanded into a book, *Parkinson's Law or the Pursuit of Progress* (1958). Based on his experience in the civil service, his book demonstrated how shallow and unnecessary the culture of working long hours really is. Kenneth Blanchard and Spenser Johnson (*The One Minute Manager*, 1981) saw the problem too. 'I'm a One Minute Manager. I call myself that because it takes very little time for me to get very big results from people.' Their book shows how to overcome the problem of misallocating time by focusing on just three key tasks – goals, praise and reprimands – all in bites of no more than a minute.

Napoleon Hill's seventh and eighth steps to acquiring riches are concerned with time management, decisiveness and avoiding procrastination. Hill's analysis of the seriously wealthy disclosed the fact that 'every one of them had the habit of reaching decisions promptly, and changing these decisions slowly, if and when they were changed at all.'

Validity today

There is little doubt that the problem of time being wasted or misspent is near universal and is unlikely to be solved in any permanent sense. To that extent Koch's ideas and Pareto's 80/20 rule seem set to be around a while yet. That said, Koch's anecdotal approach will inevitably age and be replaced, much as Hill's has been.

John Kotter

By Clive Hemingway

Name: John Paul Kotter

Born: 1947

Expertise: Leadership and change

Known for: His eight-step process for leading change

Best-known titles: *Leading Change* (1996); also see the following 'Best of HBR' papers by Kotter in *Harvard Business Review*: 'What Leaders Really Do' (Dec 2001); 'Leading Change: Why Transformation Efforts Fail' (Jan 2007); 'Choosing Strategies for Change' (Jul–Aug 2008)

Who is John Kotter?

Kotter is Konosuke Matsushita professor of leadership, emeritus, at Harvard Business School (HBS). He has held professorial tenure since his was 33 – a remarkably young age for the holder of such a position. His research has framed management thinking on leadership and change since then. Although retired from academic life, he shows no sign of slowing down – his new enterprise, Kotter International, aims to 'guide, educate, and inspire people to become better leaders, to successfully transform organizations that enrich lives today and build a better world for future generations'.

What is Kotter known for?

Following his early appointment to the faculty at Harvard Business School, Kotter's work focused on managers, rather than leaders, culminating in his paper 'General managers are not generalists' (*Harvard Business Review*, 1982). Later, his research output focused more on leadership, and how leaders effect change. This work, based on studies of successful and unsuccessful attempts at business change, culminated in Kotter's 'eight steps', which first appeared in *Harvard Business Review* in 1995 and were expanded into his bestselling book, *Leading Change*, published the following year. His subsequent work has developed individual steps, but the steps themselves remain as the cornerstone of his leadership thinking.

Kotter has expounded the eight steps through talks, short magazine articles, academic papers and management books. He has also converted the eight steps into a fable-style book (*Our Iceberg is Melting*), believing that his audience will retain more through this storytelling approach than through bald rhetoric.

The concepts

Kotter observed that many of the companies he studied were mature, and were faced with a need to undergo change in order to remain competitive in changing marketplaces. He found that most were not able to make the necessary transformations effectively, so he developed a methodology to guide such companies through change – the eight steps.

Kotter's eight steps

	What is involved	Symptoms of not completing this step
Setting the stage		
Establishing a sense of urgency	Examining market and competitive realities. Identifying and discussing crises, potential crises, or major opportunities	Paralyzed management
Forming a powerful guiding coalition	Assembling a group with enough power to lead the change effort. Encouraging the group to work together as a team	Lack of teamwork; insufficient buy-in
Deciding what to do		
Creating a vision	Creating a vision to help direct the change effort. Developing strategies for achieving that vision	Plenty of plans, but no unifying end-goal
Making it happen		
Communicating the vision	Using every vehicle possible to communicate the new vision and strategies. Teaching new behaviors by the example of the guiding coalition	Communication done in a 'fire-and-forget' manner, without ongoing progress reporting. Communicators themselves not yet bought in to the transformation

Empowering others to act on the vision	Getting rid of obstacles to change. Changing systems or structures that seriously undermine the vision. Encouraging risk taking and non-traditional ideas, activities and actions	Anti-change personnel, possibly senior, remain in-post
Planning for and creating short-term wins	Planning for visible performance improvements. Creating those improvements	Urgency (engendered in Step 1) declines
Consolidating improvements and producing still more change	Using increased credibility to change systems, structures and policies that don't fit the vision. Hiring, promoting and developing employees who can implement the vision. Reinvigorating the process with new projects, themes and change agents	Transformation process perceived as a finite task – once the process ends, old habits resurface
Making it stick		
Institutionalizing new approaches	Articulating the connections between new behaviors and corporate success. Developing the means to ensure leadership development and succession.	Successors chosen unwisely, so new culture not properly embedded

(Adapted from JP Kotter, 'Leading Change: Why Transformation Efforts Fail', Harvard Business Review, *March–April 1995, pp. 59–67.)*

Kotter argues that failure of business change results from skimping or omitting one or more steps, or tackling the steps in the wrong order. He observes that managers will be particularly prone to skimping on a step as they seek to complete tasks quickly, but that this is ultimately counter-productive.

Strength of leadership is emphasized as an acute requirement for successful completion of many steps. The sense of urgency for change involves taking people out of their comfort zones in order to face up to a crisis. The building of a coalition will need strong leadership if everyone is going to buy in to the change. Arguably, a hallmark of strong leadership is the ability to set out a vision. Disposing of obstacles (incompatible systems, employees who resist the change) takes bold, confident leadership. Anchoring the changes, thereby avoiding regression to the 'old ways', is another leadership role.

Kotter's body of work pre- and post-development of the eight steps adopts a very practical approach, as though this is a toolkit for a leader faced with a looming business transformation. For example, if you want to know how to remove obstacles to change, Kotter has the answer – identify the sort of resistance encountered, and choose an appropriate strategy to deal with it (education/communication, participation/involvement, facilitation/support, negotiation/agreement, manipulation/co-option and explicit/implicit coercion).

Most recently, Kotter has concentrated on what he considers to be the most difficult step – creating a sense of urgency (Step 1). In earlier work, he thought that the 'burning platform' was a good way to do this – paint a picture of impending crisis, or better still get someone on Wall Street to paint the picture for you. More recently, he has modified his view to add that increasing contact with the outside world is best, and that this can be achieved by sending managers out to spend time with customers, or by inviting customers in to talk to the company. Kotter finds that exposing company people to their customers enables them to realize for themselves when change has become necessary, for example when a product no longer meets customer expectations. He advocates taking video of these encounters to show around the company. (For more on this, see JP Kotter (2008) *A Sense of Urgency,* Harvard Business School Press).

How real companies use Kotter's concepts

Publicly quoted companies can be guarded about discussing their change programs, as such comments can fuel speculation and materially affect their share price. However, the following companies have allowed their cases to be described on the Kotter International website.

Red Robin – a restaurant chain – set out to reduce the time for new restaurants to achieve normalization from 36 months to six months. The source of the urgency was financial. The vision is particularly simple ('Give guests what they ordered, when they ordered it, in a timely and respectful manner'), but kept the company focused on its core business. Perhaps the key step in this case was the empowerment of the staff, achieved by improving the proficiency and variety of skills that employees acquired through a revised training regime. This enabled the vision and the change goal to be achieved, along with reduced staff turnover. The change in culture was not restricted to the restaurants – back-office functions were also transformed.

Norfolk Southern – a rail freight terminal operation – wanted to improve safety as a means of improving efficiency. The major obstacle was a culture that considered that a certain level of accidental injuries was acceptable. A particular problem in this case was communications, as many employees are crewing trains and not able to process email or listen to audio broadcasts while working. Leadership changed the vision to one of injury-free operations. In consequence, communication about change was added to staff briefings that were held at the start of shifts. This ensured that staff were regularly exposed to messages. In these messages, the reason for the change was styled as 'an appeal to the heart', in which staff were asked to consider the risks not only to themselves, but to their families. This helped the safety messages to get across.

Centrelink – an Australian social services agency newly created from two pre-existing organizations – urgently needed to establish itself. The CEO used the eight steps to achieve this, primarily using a powerful coalition to promote and instill her new vision. Despite a very wide-ranging brief, the coalition group was quite formalized, with regular meetings to raise (and resolve) issues and inform each other on the status of work in progress. The coalition was large (about 100 people, from an organization of 23,000 employees) and potentially unwieldy, but the CEO considered that the benefits of debate in a large forum yielded sound strategy.

How it dovetails with other guru theories

Kurt Lewin, writing in 1947, viewed change as a three-step process: 'Unfreeze – Move (i.e. change) – Refreeze'. Kotter agrees with the first two stages, but applies a different meaning to the 'refreezing' advocated by Lewin. For Lewin, it was a new system or structure that underwent refreezing once in place. These new systems and structures will themselves become obsolete in time, necessitating a repeat of the 'Unfreeze – Move – Refreeze' process. For Kotter, the refreezing is applied to a cultural change, with the intention that the organization will continue to evolve in response to the demands placed on it.

Kotter (and some other 1990s writers) subscribes to the 'rational philosophy' of change, in that it is leaders within organizations who stimulate change. This is only one of at least 10 philosophies of change. The others are as follows.

- **Biological philosophy:** advocates that organizations undergo externally driven natural selection, and it is quite normal for some to age and die over time, while others adapt to changes in their environment.
- **Institutional philosophy:** in which change is man-made, but triggered by events outside the organization, such as legislation. As businesses conform to these pressures, they adopt similarities, such as in their corporate structures.
- **Resource philosophy:** which states that change arises from the organization's pursuit of the resources (including people) that it needs to function. Unlike the institutional philosophy, resource philosophy urges businesses to distinguish themselves, by seeking unique assets.
- **Contingency philosophy:** which contends that change arises as organizations juggle their technology, strategy, structure, systems, style and culture in search of increased efficiency.
- **Psychological philosophy:** which concerns changes in the feelings of individuals within organizations, and contends that these feelings change more slowly than the pace of change within organizations, leading to discomfort.
- **Political philosophy:** which assumes that organizations change so as to increase the power of internal individuals or groups. This is strongly internally driven, so much so

that external pressures for change may be ignored. Kotter urges the formation of powerful coalitions, but the Kotter coalitions are constructed and directed by the leader.

- **Cultural philosophy:** which is concerned with the shared experience of change (*cf* the psychological philosophy, which concerns the individual). Cultural change involves changing an organization's values, which may be deeply entrenched, and difficult to move.
- The **systems view** of organizations paints them as composed of rational, inter-related units. Changing one unit will therefore affect other units, so change should be viewed holistically.
- Perhaps the most complex and abstract is the **postmodern philosophy**, which contends that discourse builds our (different) worlds and realities, and is behind changes to those worlds.

Validity today

Kotter's eight steps share much with the 1990s change management thinking, in that change is viewed as difficult, but there is no reason why it can't be done successfully if you follow a few golden rules in the right order. Change management thinking has itself changed since the 1990s in some very important ways. First, although it was recognized that change affects and is effected by people, it was assumed that people could and should be made to carry out change programs, and if it turned out that anyone wasn't committed to the cause, then they should be dispensed with. Second, and related to the first, is that change is driven by a visionary leader – ergo change is a top-down process.

Modern, transcendental leaders operate more inclusively and democratically than their predecessors, and the 1990s notion of staff as automatons is becoming less popular. The 1990s image of loyal subjects deploying a leader's change program is fading, and being replaced by one where change is effected more organically, by the widest cross section of the workforce.

Kotter seems to make a bridge between 1990s and current thinking. He stresses the importance of a visionary leader, but also urges buy-in and active participation from all involved. Although a stepwise process, Kotter recognizes that change should be a continuous and integral part of the organizational culture. This is an advance on the 'Unfreeze – Move – Refreeze' thinking.

See Kotter's blog at http://blogs.forbes.com/johnkotter/ and his website at www.kotterinternational.com.

Tom Peters

By Colin Barrow

Name: Thomas J Peters

Born: 1942

Expertise: His seminal work *In Search of Excellence* has defined Peters as an expert in personal and business empowerment and problem solving methodologies

Known for: McKinsey 7S model: writings on business organizations and strategic practices, including identification of eight common themes as being the critical factors in determining excellent performance in a business enterprise

Best-known titles: *In Search of Excellence* (1982, co-authored with Robert H Waterman, Jr); *A Passion for Excellence* (1985, co-authored with Nancy Austin); *Thriving on Chaos* (1987); *Liberation Management* (1992); *The Pursuit of WOW!* (1994); *Re-imagine! Business Excellence in a Disruptive Age* (2003); *Trends* (2005, co-authored with Martha Barletta); *The Little Big Things: 163 Ways to Pursue Excellence* (2010)

Who is Tom Peters?

Peters served in the US Navy both in Vietnam and later at the Pentagon, where he developed an interest in military strategy, in the civilian branch of which he became a renowned expert. He is a civil engineering graduate of Cornell and earned an MBA and PhD in business at Stanford.

From 1974 to 1981 Peters worked as a management consultant at McKinsey & Company, where he garnered the material for *In Search of Excellence*. Since 1978, when the work on *Search* began, Peters estimates that he's given over 2,500 speeches, flown 5,000,000 miles, spoken before 3,000,000 people and presented in 48 states and 63 countries. The book itself has sold over six million copies and variously been described as 'a landmark book' and 'the greatest business book of all time', and rated by the *New York Times* as the book of the century.

What is Peters known for?

While at McKinsey, Peters began work on a structure and people project as part of a major piece of work and at the heart of the company's expertise. In 1979 Peters, at the request of McKinsey's Munich office, presented his findings to Siemens in a 700-slide two-day seminar. A two-day brainstorming session with Tony Athos, a professor at the Harvard Business School, in 1980 turned 'our ramblings', as Peters described their work to-date, into something 'crisp' and memorable. The '7-S framework', the cornerstone of the research behind *In Search of Excellence*, was unveiled in an article in *Business Horizons* later that year. (RH Waterman Jr, TJ Peters and JR Phillips (1980) 'Structure is not organization', *Business Horizons* 23(3): 14). This framework was developed into the eight attributes that emerged to characterize the excellent companies described in the book.

The concepts

The concept behind the theory is what came to be known as the McKinsey 7-S model.

McKinsey 7-S model

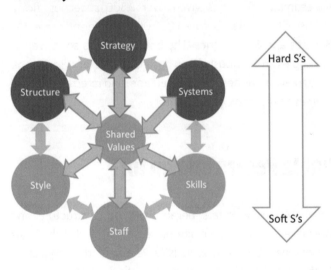

Despite shared values — or the 'superordinate goal', as Peters also refers to it — usually being placed at the centre of any diagrammatic representation of the model, there was no precedence among the seven Ss.

- **Structure:** the way a business is managed usually set out in an organization chart showing who reports to whom.

- **Strategy:** the actions a business performs or plans to execute to meet completion and any other changes in the external environment.
- **Systems:** the routine procedures and processes used to underpin the structure and strategy.
- **Style:** refers to the way in which the organization is led and managed.
- **Skills:** corporate strengths and distinctive competences – what the firm is renowned for.
- **Staff:** covers the HR function and the way that people are recruited, inducled and developed.
- **Shared values:** these are the core values of the company that describe corporate culture and the way everyone is expected to behave. Toys 'R' Us Inc, for example, describes its values as being rapid, real, reliable and responsible. It believes this will enable it to best serve its customers, employees, shareholders, communities and kids.

All seven Ss need to be kept in view all the time, otherwise less than excellent performance can be expected. Initially the authors saw a division between the 'hard Ss' (strategy, structure and systems) that are theoretically easily described, and the 'soft Ss' (style, skills and staff) that at first seemed less easy to describe and more fluid. Peters' claims that his subsequent work can best be captured in six words: 'Hard is soft. Soft is hard.' His thesis here is that numbers can give a false appearance of precision, quoting as an example the sky-high soundness scores that the ratings agencies gave to packages of dubious mortgages; whilst staff (people), shared values (corporate culture) and skills (core competencies) are 'the bedrock on upon which the adaptive and enduring enterprise is built'.

Taking the 7-S model as their starting point, Peters and his co-author hunted out excellent companies from which to distill

'Lessons from America's Best-Run Companies', as the book's strapline put it. The companies shortlisted for investigation were drawn from those that had performed well over the preceding two decades, measured by six yardsticks: compound asset growth, compound equity growth, ratio of market value to book value, average return on total capital, average return on equity and average return on sales. There has been much debate over whether these measures are sufficient – they only measure financial performance and ignore measures such as brand value, seen by many as a vital measure of excellence. Even in the financial arena such crucial areas as free cash flow and gearing were ignored.

Peters didn't completely load the deck in his favor by only picking sure-fire winners. Starting with a list of 62 firms they removed 20 of what they saw as being the less resilient. Whilst the remaining companies were all sizeable, only three ranked among the top 25 by sales on the New York Stock Exchange. Only 22 were among the 500 largest. Many, including the star of the book, the computer company IBM, faltered soon after. Some, like the cheap airline People Express, went bust.

The authors went on to develop eight themes for their study, whittled down from the unwieldy 22 they started out with.

1. **A bias for action:** that is, 'getting on with it', rather than being paralyzed by introspective navel gazing.
2. **Closeness to the customer:** listening to and learning from the people served by the business.
3. **Autonomy and entrepreneurship:** fostering creativity, being tolerant of mistakes and nurturing leaders and champions.
4. **Productivity through people:** treating employees as a valuable resource delivering quality and improvements in productivity.

5. **Hands-on, value-driven:** a management philosophy that states what the business stands for and can be used to guide everyday actions in a practical manner.
6. **Stick to the knitting:** stay as close as possible with the business that you know for most of what you do for most of the time.
7. **Simple form:** a few layers of management and lean headquarters staff.
8. **Simultaneous loose–tight properties:** with power devolved to the front line where possible and practical, but adopting centralized values.

How real companies use Peters' concepts

In essence, the whole book is about how real companies used the strategies identified as being the source of excellence. The real test is whether the strategies identified in the book have worked over the longer term. An article by Dan Ackman, a Forbes.com journalist, tracked the performance of the 'excellent' companies over the 20 years after the book came out, a symmetrical period to the 20 years of history used as criteria for selection. By then 24 of the firms were among the largest 500 public companies. One thousand pounds invested in the Excellence Index, had such as thing existed, would have yielded £14,000, compared to just £8,500 for the US stock market as a whole.

So much for history – who follows these rules today? Take one of the most powerful messages from the Peters study – 'stick to the knitting'. Pepsi Cola, a great company by any measure, is a company driven by growth at all costs. Its goal is 15% revenue growth long term and in pursuit of this it owns (or has owned) the world's largest snack food company and three of the seven largest fast food chains in the US: Pizza Hut, Taco Bell and KFC. The sun never sets on a PepsiCo restaurant. But despite outselling its rival, Coca-Cola, $43bn to $31bn in 2010, it is valued at just $102bn. Coca-Cola, in contrast, was valued at $120bn, a premium of nearly 20% and attributed in investment circles to the company largely sticking to its beverage heritage. Neither of those companies was in the Peters study, but McDonald's, another great and successful business, was. On McDonald's silver anniversary in 1980, it had 6,263 restaurants in 27 countries. By May 2011 it had more than 32,000 restaurants serving approximately 64 million customers in 117 countries each day.

How it dovetails with other guru theories

In Search of Excellence draws on the work of almost every significant business thinker either to support its arguments or to refute past ideas. Frederick Winslow Taylor (*The Principles of Scientific Management*, 1911), whose obsession with efficiency measures was considered to have completely overshadowed less quantifiable social values – the soft Ss in the McKinsey model. Alfred Chandler (*Strategy and Structure: Chapters in the History of the American Industrial Enterprise*, MIT Press, 1969), whose research based on four case studies of American conglomerates that dominated their industry from the 1920s onward ruled that structure should always follow strategy. Peters' study of excellent companies found this rarely to be the case in the wider and more current business world. In any event, he noted that the 'crucial problems in strategy were more often those of execution and continuous adaption: getting it done, staying flexible'. Peter Drucker, though quoted favorably in places, was dismissed as someone who by the late 1970s had played a role in getting the great American corporation 'run by bean counters'. Elton Mayo (*The Human Problems of an Industrialized Civilization*, 1933) and Chester Barnard (*The Functions of the Executive*, 1968) were seen as being on the right track in recognizing that an organization has to satisfy the motives of its members whilst aiming to achieve specific goals, if it is to survive and prosper.

There have been plenty of ideas to challenge the *In Search of Excellence* approach, three of which stand out.

In 1994 Xerox related business excellence to a certification process where it defined excellence as scoring high on the following six excellence criteria, none of which conflict with the 7 Ss.

1. Management leadership
2. Human resource management
3. Business process management
4. Customer and market focus
5. Information utilization and quality tools
6. Business results

The balanced scorecard, developed by Robert Kaplan and David Norton and published in a *Harvard Business Review* article in 1992, set out a way to align business activities to the vision and strategy of the organization, improve internal and external communications and monitor organizational performance against strategic goals. Its uniqueness was to add non-financial performance measures to traditional financial targets to give managers and directors a more 'balanced' view of organizational performance. Although Kaplan and Norton are credited with coining the phrase, the idea of a 'balanced scorecard' originated with General Electric's work on performance measurement reporting in the 1950s and the work of French process engineers (who created the *tableau de bord* – literally, a 'dashboard' of performance measures) in the early part of the 20th century.

In 2001 an internal Toyota document set out what became known as the Toyota Way – the 4 Ps. Four categories, all starting with 'P' – philosophy, process, people/partners and problem solving – were broken down into 14 management principles that underpinned its success. None of these would cause Peters or his co-author much concern. 'Develop exceptional people and teams who follow your company's philosophy' (principle 10) fits well with any of the soft Ss in the McKinsey model. Principle 12, 'Go and see for yourself to thoroughly understand the situation', is a dead ringer for 'MBWA – management by walking about', a principle endorsed by several of the excellent companies in the Peters study.

Validity today

When challenged on the long-term validity of the ideas outlined in their book, the authors note:

> Both of us have done a great deal of writing since *Excellence*, and we've expressed what we've seen in different terms. But we've never done better than in this book. The attributes are just that: attributes, not principles. But until something clearly better comes along, we'll stick with these.

Peters acknowledges the role played by Tony Athos, the Harvard Business School professor who led the brainstorming session that produced the 7-S model, for its longevity.

Tony was insistent that, corny as it appeared to be, we develop an alliterative model - find stuff that began with 'S' in this case. In retrospect, it was a move of near genius. In my opinion, without the alliteration, which I initially found juvenile, the concept would not have been the sort being touted almost 30 years later.

Michael Porter

By Trudi Knight

Name: Michael Eugene Porter

Born: 1947

Expertise: Leading authority on competitive strategy and the concept of competitive advantage. Currently a professor at the Harvard Business School

Known for: Porter has made several pivotal contributions to management thinking, the most famous being competitive advantage

Best-known titles: *Competitive Strategy: Techniques for Analyzing Industries and Competitors* (1980); *Competitive Advantage: Creating and Sustaining Superior Performance* (1985); *The Competitive Advantage of Nations* (1990); *On Competition* (1998)

Who is Michael Porter?

Michael Porter is regarded by many as the leading business guru of modern business strategy. Over the past three decades he has continued to break new ground and win accolades. In addition to his academic work, Porter founded Monitor Company, one of the world's very best strategic management consultancies, where he continues to work. He has advised business, government, and the social sector, serving as strategy adviser to leading international companies including Caterpillar, Procter & Gamble, and Royal Dutch Shell.

What is Porter known for?

Porter's 1980s work was revolutionary. It provided truly practical frameworks for thinking strategically. His first book, *Competitive Strategy* (1980), focused on industry and brought the analytical rigor of microeconomics to strategy. It introduced structures to enable managers to analyze industry attractiveness and competitive positioning. Put another way, it enables business people to scratch deep beneath the surface of their marketplace to uncover real and under-exploited opportunities. *Competitive Strategy* substantially increased awareness of the subject among academic and business communities and continues to provide the foundation of strategic thinking to this day.

His second book, *Competitive Advantage*, published in 1985, was equally influential. This companion to *Competitive Strategy* looked at how a firm can create and sustain competitive advantage in its marketplace. In it Porter set out a system he had developed to look 'inside the firm' at what resources it had and how they were used, for identifying advantages against the competition. In the 25 years plus of widespread acceptance since, these fundamental concepts of competitive advantage and sustainable competitive advantage have become the established methods in this area.

Together, these books transformed strategic thinking by developing three linked concepts: the 'five forces', 'generic strategy' and 'value chain' frameworks. Today these concepts remain at the heart of most business school strategy courses. Beyond these two seminal works, Porter has made other lasting contributions to strategy, increasing both its academic rigor and its accessibility to managers. This impressive accomplishment has not been equalled before or since, so that 30 years after his first seminal contribution, Porter's work continues to provide remarkable insights into the nature of competition and strategy.

The concepts

The concept of competitive advantage identifies and defines the strategic goals of an organization. Porter suggests that the goal of every firm is to achieve a competitive advantage over its rivals. To do this it either sells at a lower cost or differentiates its product from that of its competitors.

By obtaining a competitive advantage, Porter argues, a firm can earn profits that are higher than the average profit earned by competitors within the industry (what he calls 'excess profits'). However, he suggests that achieving a competitive advantage is one thing, but to sustain this advantage is more difficult. A sustainable competitive advantage is one that cannot be duplicated or imitated by other firms entering the industry in the long run and allows a company to compete for the excess profits enjoyed by existing firms.

Porter proposes that business strategy is the fundamental basis of sustainable competitive advantage for a business. A business's strategy is a deliberate search for a plan of action that will develop its competitive advantage and compound it. To enable an organization to devise such a strategy Porter developed the following frameworks:

- five forces
- generic strategies
- value chain.

Together these frameworks help to understand where the organization is in its lifecycle and where it might seek to develop in the future. Here's a quick summary, with the key points for you to apply in today's business world.

Five forces

Porter's five forces is a simple yet powerful framework that helps organizations identify the strength of the five market levers: suppliers, customers, potential new entrants, substitutes (being alternative products that serve the same purpose) and existing competitive rivalry. By knowing the strength of each force, management can decide how to influence or exploit particular characteristics of their market. For example, if the bargaining strength of customers is high (same product offered by a number of companies), to reduce this, a company could consider partnering with other competitors or perhaps provide incentives enticing new customers.

The five forces framework

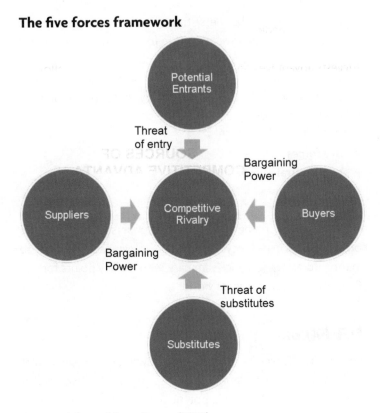

Source: Adapted from Porter (1980)

When evaluating what strategy to follow, Porter has three generic options organizations can pursue for achieving above-average performance. These can be seen as an extension to the five forces analysis, and help determine where an organization should position itself against competitors.

Generic strategies

Porter suggests achieving competitive advantage requires a firm to make a choice about which type of advantage it should try to achieve, as well as how. Being 'all things to all people' is a recipe for strategic mediocrity and below-average performance, and often results in a firm having no competitive advantage at all. He suggests advantage can accrue by choosing one of the following generic strategies.

Porter's generic strategies

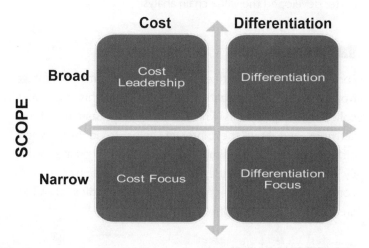

Source: Porter (1980)

- **Cost leadership.** This is being the lowest-cost producer in the industry. This does not necessarily mean having the lowest price. The price can be the same as competitors', but by earning higher profits these can be plowed back into the business.
- **Differentiation.** This market position is where customers are willing to pay a premium price for goods or services offering added value from design, quality and service. This is often a strategy adopted by organizations that recognize they are unable to compete on price.

- **Focus.** This refers to the market focus, either directed at a niche market or aimed at a wider audience in a range of market segments.

While these generic strategies relate to competitive positioning externally, Porter suggests the advantage stems from the distinct activities a firm performs. To understand a firm's internal resources and capabilities for leveraging competitive advantage, Porter developed the value chain analysis.

Value chain

Porter's value chain identifies sources of competitive advantage from within the organization itself. He sees this chain as a collection of processes which create value. Examining firms' activities and how they interact helps to identify where differences lie. Quite simply, an organization creates value by performing its activities more cheaply or better than its competition. His value chain, including examples of value-creating activities, comprises the following.

Five primary activities
1. **Inbound logistics:** quality of components and materials.
2. **Operations:** defect-free products or operational excellence.
3. **Outbound logistics:** fast delivery or efficient order processes.
4. **Marketing:** building brand reputation.
5. **Sales services:** building brand reputation.

Four support activities
1. **Procurement:** purchasing efficiently.
2. **Technology development:** rapid, innovative new product development.

3. **Human resource management:** training to support customer service experience.
4. **Firm infrastructure:** management information system that supports fast response capabilities.

This approach can provide a greater awareness of where costs are incurred, where differences are created and how a business can make them work together. Using this analytical tool to formulate a strategy offers insight into a firm's strengths and where opportunities may be exploited (from Porter's five forces analysis) as a basis for competitive advantage.

In summary, it is clear that Porter's frameworks enable organizations to formulate and develop the most appropriate strategy to achieve competitive advantage. These analytical tools provide insight from both external (five forces) and internal (value chain) perspectives. When embarking on this process these insights are invaluable. If an organization's business strategy is to achieve a competitive advantage it must possess a clear strategic direction (generic strategies), as in today's dynamic marketplace being 'all things to all people' is not sustainable in the long run.

How real companies use Porter's concepts

Dyson Ltd is an excellent illustration of the practicalities of Porter's concepts in the business world. With an ethos that promotes 'thinking outside of the box', its focus on innovation has resulted in the creation of many products which improve on the status quo.

First came the dual cyclone bagless vacuum cleaner. More recently, the Air Blade hand dryer introduced the first significant improvements in both drying time and hygiene for decades. This product alone meant Dyson broke into the commercial market with large orders from institutions such as hospitals and service stations. To this day innovation continues to build competitive advantage for Dyson. This success story rings true with Porter's theory of 'sticking to' one generic strategy for creating advantage. In this case, being different by offering unique quality products consistently has enabled Dyson to gain an edge in its marketplace. As Porter suggests in the five forces, by effectively reducing customers' buyer power as Dyson has done by being the only company offering its products has created advantage.

And Dyson's success does not just stop at generic strategies and market forces. Along the way, Dyson has made cost savings 'inside the firm' by moving production to cheaper alternatives overseas. This allowed for the money saved to be plowed back into research and development, once again maintaining the focus on innovation. This additional research and development spend, combined with developing an aspirational brand, has added to the continued success of the company. The strengthening of its internal activities is a great example of how to convert Porter's theory of the value chain into very real competitive advantage for Dyson.

How it dovetails with other guru theories

Like Porter, many management thought leaders suggest that achieving and sustaining a competitive advantage will result in long-term success for an organization. Porter's seminal works in the 1980s on the concept of competitive advantage were a springboard for many other significant contributions from notable authors.

Recently, with an increasingly dynamic marketplace, Porter's thinking has been extended by David Aaker's *Strategic Market Management* (2007), which advanced the theory that both external and internal perspectives combined are necessary for devising strategy that delivers competitive advantage. Porter's frameworks remain to this day the primary starting point for strategic analysis.

Validity today

Not surprisingly, Porter's (1980) five forces model has some major limitations in today's business world. It is not easily able to take into account some new business models and the very rapid pace of change in certain markets such as digital technology. The value of Porter's model is more that it enables managers to think about the current situation of their industry in a structured, easy-to-understand way – and remains a very useful starting point for further analysis.

With Porter's (1980) generic strategies he states that successful organizations will select and concentrate their efforts on implementing just one of the strategies. However, it does appear that while cost leadership and differentiation may be seen as mutually exclusive, successful strategies can be based on a mix of the two. Although Porter's ideas have been questioned and debated, they nevertheless provide an extremely useful structure for analyzing industries and competitive strategy.

The concept of competitive advantage was an attempt by Porter to identify and define the strategic goals of an organization. To achieve competitive advantage Porter (in 1985) suggests analyzing the activities within the organization through the value chain. However, to succeed in today's extraordinarily fast-moving business environment it is important not to take too static or unified a view of either the environment or an organization's capabilities.

To this day, Porter's concepts are used in academic and business communities alike. His tools ensure consistency and an appropriate level of rigor and, when applied, the concepts sharpen the focus and ensure a methodical, balanced approach for making sense of this changing marketplace.

Ricardo Semler

By Modwenna Rees-Mogg

Name: Ricardo Semler

Born: 1959

Expertise: Adopting unconventional management practices to ensure a more successful, happier business

Known for: Having completely revolutionized how a business can be run, with a particular focus on liberating employees from the traditional rules of employment. Under his ownership, Semco has become one of Brazil's most successful companies, with turnover growth of 40% per annum

Best-known titles: *Maverick* (1993); *The Seven-Day Weekend* (2003)

Who is Ricardo Semler?

Son of Brazilian immigrant entrepreneur Antonio Semler, who founded Semco, Ricardo Semler is a Brazilian and is now the CEO of Semco SA. A Harvard MBA, he joined his father's company, Semco, and proceeded to completely re-engineer the business, from what it did to how it is run.

He has been named Brazil's business leader of the year twice, is vice president of the Federation of Industries of Brazil, and a board member of SOS Atlantic Forest. Today, he is frequently to be found on the international speaker circuit encouraging other business people to adopt the Semler Way.

What is Semler known for?

After conflict with his father about which management style Semco should adopt, in 1980 Ricardo threatened to leave. His father reacted by resigning and vesting ownership of the company to his son when he was 21. On his first day Ricardo fired 60% of the company's top managers and proceeded to save the then struggling company. At 25 he suffered from a fainting spell, which encouraged him to seek a new way of operating the business so that he and his employees could have a better work-life balance.

His first attempt at creating a more decentralized management structure using a matrix organizational structure failed, but in the late 1980s, following the success of the Nucleus of Technological Innovation unit at Semco — a unit designed to develop new business and product lines, which identified 18 opportunities in its first six months — Semler instated satellite units throughout the business which rapidly grew to be responsible for two-thirds of activity.

Despite the hyperinflation in Brazil in the early 1990s, Semco thrived. Thanks to full employee engagement, the company took the necessary steps to avoid failure, including up to 40% wage cuts for management and employees in return for profit sharing arrangements and giving employees the right to approve every item of expenditure. Employees and management were also encouraged to move around the company, taking many different roles to get a better understanding of operations. There were dramatic improvements in operational performance and equally dramatic improvements in profitability.

Once the Brazilian economy started to recover, Semco's performance took off. It has grown from a sub $5m turnover company in the 1980s to one with sales in excess of $400m in the early 2000s. This has been achieved by considerable diversification into value-added service-led business activities in areas ranging from manufacturing to venture capital. Semco also has interests in other businesses worth approximately $9bn. Semco has never been afraid of change. In the last decade it has divested a number of its operations and has set up partnerships with companies such as Pitney Bowes, GMF Gouda, H&R Block Inc and Loedige.

The concepts

Semler's theories invert almost every conventional business practice. Outlined below are a handful of his better known ideas, all of which he deployed within Semco.

The seven-day weekend

The eponymous title of his second book, Semler advocates that if employees take their work home even if only to check their emails, then why should they not be entitled to take their private life into work? This means allowing staff to choose their own hours of work and even where they work. Semco also has a deal 'retire a little' with its staff, whereby they can take part of their retirement early (e.g. one day a week now) in return for agreeing to work the equivalent amount of time after retirement. The philosophy is that people will be most productive for the company if they are given the freedom to take responsibility for their own lives and achieve a work-life balance that suits them. He believes that this does not make people carefree, but in fact more responsible, and it also reduces stress levels, one of the biggest reasons for employee failure in today's world.

Equality for everyone

Semco's staff can have business cards or not, depending on whether they need them or not for business purposes. They can also choose their own job titles on the same basis. They do not have fixed desks or offices and only keep their jobs if their peer group declares a need for them. Semco does not even have a head office, as Semler believes this creates a sense of hierarchy; staff operate from a series of satellite offices, based around Sao Paolo originally, and now in three countries.

Junior and senior staff are placed next to one another so they can learn from each other. Managers are appointed by the staff who will work for them, and those who do not perform are voted out by those same people. Board meetings have two open places which employees can sign up for on a first come, first served basis. Everyone at board meetings is expected to contribute to the meeting. Decisions made at meetings must be by majority vote, not by the influence of the most important person. Even though he is majority owner of Semco, Semler endeavors not to make any decisions at all, trusting his staff to come out with the right answers for the business and themselves. He still has the right to come up with ideas and make suggestions, but has to accept the outcome if these are turned down by the rest of the team.

No hierarchy of reward; full competition for roles

At Semco, people who do not fit in a role are invited to try out others. It may take several attempts for them to find a role that fits, but this is worth it if it allows them to out-perform overall. No-one has the right to a more senior job just because of time served. Jobs are rotated regularly (including, sometimes, the role of CEO), which means that there is no sense of a right to a specific job, unless you continue to be the best person to undertake it. The corollary is that there should be a job that suits everyone, somewhere within the organization.

People are regularly hired from outside the company, but internal candidates are given a 30% advantage in the application process (in terms of scoring who is most suitable for the role) because it is assumed that they understand the Semco way better than an external candidate.

Control is bad; trust is all

Staff at Semco do not have their emails checked by the company – at all! They are free to explore new business with customers and to find new ways of winning new business from potential customers. Staff are trusted to find their own routes to achieving their set objectives, even if this means that established methods are over-ridden. Semler believes this approach frees employees to make decisions that will get the best outcomes in a continuously changing world.

Replace long-term planning; take a six-month view

Semler says that you should not try to plan for the long term or you risk chasing a business stream that will eventually die. You should only plan for the next six months. This may mean changing the results you require. However, he believes in giving both people and projects every opportunity to succeed, including funding loss-making projects for years if necessary; the only proviso is that there are regular reviews to see if this is still the right strategy to follow.

Success is more important than money; passion is most important of all

Semler is passionate that while the purpose of being in business is to run it profitably, achieving results for the sake of monetary reward is self-limiting. It is more important to achieve a successful outcome than just to make a lot of money. Those purely motivated by money are led by greed, making a volatile business which is hard to control. A business motivated by successful outcomes for the customers, suppliers and staff creates a sustainable business headed in the right direction. But money should not be ignored; it is critical to chase profitable business and deliver superior results to justify the charges made.

Learning; not training

Semco employees are encouraged to learn all the time; the company offers lots of routes to learn, including its 'rush hour

MBA' where staff teach each other about what they have learned. Training is not focused upon – instead employees are encouraged to 'amble and ramble' as they work out the best way to do their jobs.

Long-term relationships and a partnership approach

Semco is adamant that it will not do business where there is any hint of corruption, particularly bribery. Even if a contract is worth millions of dollars, it will decline to accept the work if the bidding process has involved a kickback, for example. Companies should aim to build really long-term relationships with customers, suppliers and partners.

Semco aims to build long-term relationships with its employees who are properly engaged with a partnership approach. This may include looking at new ways to work with staff, including if necessary allowing them to purchase assets from the company and then subcontract with Semco to deliver services using those assets. This philosophy also permits giving staff unlimited time off, if required, to deal with personal issues such as family illness. Semco also endeavors to find solutions which will leave ex-employees with a positive attitude to the company; on occasion this has included writing off debts incurred by failing employees, rather than chasing them for the money, after they leave.

Win difficult, complicated-to-deliver business; not low-hanging fruit

This is a key competitive protection for Semco. It focuses on winning business that others already, and will continue to, find difficult and expensive to deliver. By delivering efficient and better results for these activities than its competitors, Semco can achieve premium pricing for the contracts it obtains.

Growth is not necessarily the route to success

Semler takes the view that a business unit can reach an optimum size and position. Growth thereafter may be detrimental. Semler believes that if you follow the logic of perpetual growth, you will end up with a handful of monolithic enterprises and this is the opposite of what is required to generate growth – namely, innovation and enterprise.

Despite all this, systems are important

The underlying theme of Semler's management style is about finding better ways and processes to achieve a superior outcome. By preventing rigid structures in a business it is able to flex itself to meet changing market conditions. It also creates a competitive, peer-led pressure to perform, which probably explains why the company has performed outstandingly well over decades.

How real companies use Semler's concepts

As Semler's concepts are so unconventional and are impossible to implement to make a quick difference, they are not usually adopted by other businesses, although the principles of greater freedom for employees, with the obvious corollary of judgement only on performance, is a theme that many companies are paying increasing attention to.

How it dovetails with other guru theories

Semler's strategies are typically seen as maverick, as the title of his first book suggests. However, the underlying principles of his management style still involve having an ordered business which chases the most profitable business it can from customers with which it has long-term relationships. Like most gurus, he believes that a business needs to have a strong moral underpinning to succeed.

Validity today

With the global economic crisis refusing to go away and with people living longer than ever, Semler's philosophies resonate perhaps more than at any time in recent history.

Challenging assumptions, 360° management and employee empowerment, prioritization of the customer, close attention to cost control and encouraging flexibility of thought have never been more important than in today's business world.

Peter Senge

By Colin Barrow

Name: Peter Senge

Born: 1947

Expertise: Senge is renowned as an expert on organizational development and presented a series of works on how dynamic organizations continuously adapt and improve

Known for: He has encapsulated his vision of the 'learning organization' in a series of titles, the best known of which is *The Fifth Discipline*

Best-known titles: *The Fifth Discipline – the Art and Practice of the Learning Organization* (1990; 2nd edn 2006); *The Fifth Discipline Fieldbook: Strategies and Tools for Building a Learning Organization* (1994), co-authored with Charlotte Roberts, Rick Ross, Bryan Smith and Art Kleiner; *The Dance of Change: The Challenges to Sustaining Momentum in Learning Organizations* (March 1999) co-authored with George Roth; *Schools That Learn: A Fifth Discipline Fieldbook for Educators, Parents and Everyone Who Cares About Education* (2000), co-authored with Nelda H Cambron-McCabe, Timothy Lucas, Bryan Smith, Janis Dutton and Art Kleiner; *Presence: Human Purpose and the Field of the Future* (2004), co-authored with Claus Otto Scharmer, Joseph Jaworski and Betty Sue Flowers

Who is Peter Senge?

Senge has a BS in Engineering from Stanford University, an MS in Social Systems Modelling and a PhD in Management from MIT (Massachusetts Institute of Technology), where he is a senior lecturer. He has been named by *The Journal of Business Strategy* (September/October 1999) as one of the 24 people who had the greatest influence on business strategy over the last 100 years, by *The Financial Times* (2000) as one of the world's 'top management gurus', and rated by *Business Week* (October 2001) as one of the top (10) management gurus.

What is Senge known for?

Senge was virtually unknown outside the academic world until he laid down the foundation showing organizations how to use five disciplines to ensure continued growth and prosperity. His starting point is that no firm, however big or apparently successful, is guaranteed to survive for long, yet alone prosper. He quotes a number of studies demonstrating that the average life of a Fortune 500 company was around 40 years, less than a typical working life and short enough for the chances to be 50/50 that one of his readers will see their present firm disappear during their career. The central questions Senge sets out to answer are: how can companies that have excelled and reached the top collapse suddenly, drawing on examples such as People Express Airlines, one of Tom Peters' 'excellent companies'; and on the contrary, why do other companies survive and prosper? The answer to the dilemma is that the companies that survive have in some important measure succeeded in creating a 'learning organization'.

The concepts

Senge starts by explaining his disciplines with the concept of 'a lever' – the point where even modest and manageable efforts can make major differences. Here he introduces the framework of his approach, listing five disciplines of the learning organization as being the key to creating an enduringly successful venture. The first four, personal mastery, mental models, building shared vision and team learning are shown as the core (see figure below), with systems thinking as the fifth discipline – the one positioned in the centre, turning them into a logical body of theory and practice.

Senge's five disciplines

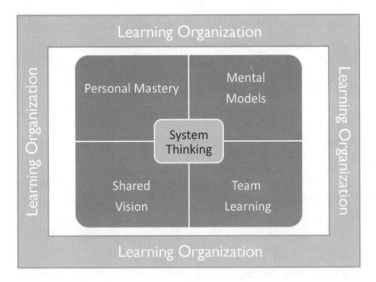

Personal mastery

Senge starts with a quote from Bill O'Brian, former President of Hanover Insurance.

> **People enter business as bright, well-educated, high-energy people, full of energy and desire to make a difference. By the time they are 30, a few are on the fast track and the rest 'put in their time' to do what matters to them on the weekend. They lose the commitment, the sense of mission, and the excitement with which they started their careers. We get damn little of their energy and almost none of their spirit.**

Personal mastery, despite overtones of macho management, has its roots in both Eastern and Western spiritual traditions. Senge describes this as the learning organization's spiritual foundation, the process of continually clarifying and deepening our personal vision, of focusing our energies, of developing patience, and of seeing reality objectively. Without this cornerstone, later disciplines, in particular building a shared vision, will be standing on shifting sand.

Mental models

The example used to introduce the second discipline is that of Royal Dutch/Shell who, according to Senge, in the early 1970s became one of the first large organizations to understand how pervasive was the influence of hidden mental models. Shell's success in the 1970s and 1980s during a period of unprecedented changes in the world oil business came in large measure from learning how to surface and challenge managers' mental models as a discipline for preparing change. Arie de Geus, Shell's coordinator of group planning during the 1980s, said that 'continuous adaptation and growth in a changing business environment depends on "institutional learning", which is the process whereby management teams change their shared mental models of the company, their markets, and their competitors. For this reason, we think of planning as learning and of corporate planning as institutional learning.'

To get to grips with these often deeply ingrained assumptions about ourselves and our organization, Senge recommends 'turning the mirror inward; learning to unearth our mental pictures of the world, to bring them to the surface and hold them rigorously to scrutiny.'

Shared vision

Whilst leaders almost invariably have personal visions for their organizations, these rarely get translated into shared visions that galvanize an organization. What has been lacking, Senge believes, is a discipline for translating vision into shared vision – 'not a "cookbook" but a set of principles and guiding practices.' Holding a shared picture or vision of the future we want to create has the power to be uplifting and to encourage experimentation and innovation. Crucially, Senge argues, it can also foster a sense of the long-term, something that is fundamental to the 'fifth discipline'. When there is a genuine vision (as opposed to the all-too-familiar 'vision statement'), people excel and learn, not because they are told to, but because they want to.

Team learning

Senge's fourth discipline states that teams collectively can have a synergistic learning value, greater than just that of the sum of the individual team members. However, you have to open the channels of communication and through learning 're-perceive the world and our relationship to it. Through learning we extend our capacity to create, to be part of the generative process of life.' But we must surmount the limitations that Senge calls the seven learning disabilities.

1. **'I am my position':** this attitude implies if I get my head down and get on everything will be okay. However, as Senge explains: 'When people in organizations focus only on their position, they have little sense of responsibility for the results produced when all positions interact.' Little proceeds exactly as planned, so cooperation is vital if the maximum learning value is to be achieved when things go wrong.

2. **'The enemy is out there':** blaming someone else when things go wrong shuts down communication and learning channels. Great leaders solve problems rather than point fingers.

3. **'The illusion of taking charge':** shoot, then aim, or as Drucker put it, 'taking action without thinking is the cause of every failure'. Thinking he saw as a function of leadership, and whilst management is doing things right, leadership is doing the right things. Face up to difficult situations, sure, but first make sure solving it will take you towards your ultimate goal.

4. **'The fixation on events':** relying too heavily on explanations that are true today but may conceal deeper patterns behind current events.

5. **'The parable of the boiled frog':** this is the much-told tale of how a frog reacts to being boiled alive. Drop it into boiling water and it will jump out and live. Bring it slowly to the boil and it won't spot the danger, and will die. The message here is that we need to be alert to subtle changes as well as to dramatic events.

6. **'The delusion of learning from experience':** experience is the best teacher, but few people in organizations directly experience the consequences of their decisions. The delivery driver who gets lost and arrives late is rarely aware of the empty supermarket shelf and the missed sales target. This

is a challenge for teams to find mechanisms for sharing knowledge rather than blame.

7. **'The myth of the management team':** Senge quotes Harvard's Chris Argyris, who showed through his research that most organizations reward those who promote the views of those further up the chain of command. Those who challenge their superiors or question corporate wisdom can expect a stunted career pattern. The organization has to get beyond this approach that dilutes thinking and eliminates challenge.

Systems thinking

Senge sees his fifth discipline as the way to integrate the other four disciplines so as to ensure decisions based solely on information from one area of an organization are not counterproductive to the system as a whole. He lists 11 laws that impinge on the fifth discipline.

1. Today's problems come from yesterday's 'solutions'.
2. The harder you push, the harder the system pushes back.
3. Behavior will grow better before it grows worse.
4. The easy way out usually leads back in.
5. The cure can be worse than the disease.
6. Faster is slower.
7. Cause and effect are not closely related in time and space.
8. Small changes can produce big results ... but the areas of highest leverage are often the least obvious.
9. You can have your cake and eat it too – but not all at once.
10. Dividing an elephant in half does not produce two small elephants.
11. There is no blame.

How real companies use Senge's concepts

The second edition of Senge's book contains 100 pages of new material on how companies are actually using and benefitting from fifth discipline practices. The 2.5 million people who have bought the book include satisfied customers such as managers at Ford, Digital, Procter & Gamble, AT&T, Herman Miller, Hanover Insurance, and Royal Dutch/Shell. The leadership development program at Nissan is based on Senge's model and is delivered by SoL (Society for Organizational Learning), a consultancy venture he heads up.

SoL's own website highlights the leadership development example of Nissan and explores the assumption that organizations need flexible workers who can deal with change and uncertainty, with personal transformation then leading directly to organizational transformation.

Nissan used the U model, a theoretical framework outlining a three-stage process for achieving deep change through perception, adaptability, creativity and innovation. The downward stroke of the U relates to 'sensing', the bottom represents 'presencing', and the upward stroke is therefore 'realizing', the point at which an organization makes the desired leap forward in its collective thinking.

As SoL's website identifies, there are three core questions at the center of Nissan's learning:

- How can we best create space for learning that integrates personal transformation with organizational transformation?

- How can we best develop the capacities in the U model in ways that ensure social technology transfer and sustained behavior change?
- What is the best 'way in' to activate the source for collective transformation?

How it dovetails with other guru theories

Senge states upfront that he assumes no credit for inventing the five disciplines; they're 'the product of the work done by hundreds of people over many years'. Senge drew extensively on the work of W Edwards Deming, remembered most for his 14-point 'system of profound knowledge', for much of his early thinking. Quoting this nugget from Deming, he credits him with saying in a sentence what he 'had struggled to put into 400 words'.

> Our prevailing system of management has destroyed our people. People are born with intrinsic motivation, self-respect, dignity, curiosity to learn, joy in learning. The forces of destruction begin with toddlers - a prize for the best Halloween customer, grades in school, gold stars - and on up through the university. On the job, people, teams, and divisions are ranked, reward for the top, punishment for the bottom.

Senge also draws on the work done by Gary Hamel and the late CK Prahalad showing the inherent failure in the strategic planning process, as generally practiced, to do much to ensure survival. With its over-emphasis on the extensive analysis of competitors' strengths and weaknesses, market niches and firms' resources, Senge concludes that typical strategic planning fails to accomplish the one worthwhile task – setting a goal that is worthy of commitment – a shared vision, the subject of the third of his five disciplines.

Senge didn't 'discover' the concept of using systems maps to explain the learning organization – in the 1950s, the concept of systems thinking was being discussed in academic circles at MIT and elsewhere. Argyris had written on the subject extensively (*Organizational Learning: A Theory of Action Perspective*, 1978). Bob Garratt, in 1999, wrote an article, 'The Learning Organization 15 years on: some personal reflections', published in a journal called *The Learning Organization*, that had itself been around since 1991. But Senge made the subject accessible to a non-academic audience. Described as an 'idealistic pragmatist', he has been able to draw on systems theory and other disciplines so that they can be worked on and applied by people in very different forms of organization.

Validity today

Senge's ideas are still popular with the wide audiences that attend seminars organized by SoL. The SoL journal, *Reflections*, in its tenth volume at the time of writing, attracts contributions from major organizations.

James Surowiecki

By Kate Walters

Name: James Michael Surowiecki

Born: 1967

Expertise: Business and finance journalism

Best known for: 'Collective wisdom' or 'collective intelligence' – the principle under which groups of people can make better decisions and estimates than individuals

Best-known titles: *The Wisdom of Crowds* (2004); *Best Business Crime Writing of the Year* (2002); Surowiecki's regular column in the *New Yorker*

Who is James Surowiecki?

James Surowiecki was a Morehead scholar at the University of North Carolina at Chapel Hill, before moving on to read for a PhD in American History at Yale. He became a financial journalist, and has written for publications including the *New York Times, Wall Street Journal, Foreign Affairs*, and *Wired*. He has been a regular writer on the *New Yorker* since 2000 and writes the 'Financial Page'.

What is Surowiecki known for?

Surowiecki's reputation continues to develop through his column in the *New Yorker*. However, he is probably still best known as the author of *The Wisdom of Crowds*. Since publication of this work, Surowiecki has been acknowledged as a leading authority on collective wisdom.

The concepts

Will a crowd come up with better decisions than a knowledgeable individual? Most of us might immediately think of bureaucracy-driven committees, in which the simplest of decisions are rendered complicated and the outcome watered down. Or even of the mob, in which the 'lowest common denominator' becomes the standard by which decisions are made and actions are carried out.

This isn't because of the inability of crowds to be effective, however, according to Surowiecki. Instead, it's because businesses and other organizations aren't aware of how to tap into the superior wisdom a crowd can provide. Indeed, the right kind of crowd can come up with solutions that are superior, or at least, more consistently superior, to those formed by the smartest of individuals.

Because of this, corporations are missing out on information, ideas, solutions and forecasts superior to those created by any superstar CEO, when the ability to access all of those is ingrained in the very fabric of the organization – the people who make it up.

This isn't to say that a CEO can simply rush onto the factory floor and lay his or her decision-making responsibilities with the staff. Surowiecki's theory rests on there being certain conditions that must be met by any wise group: diversity, independence, decentralization, and aggregation.

The most important of these conditions, arguably, is diversity. Groups made up of intelligent and not-so-intelligent members will perform better than those made up of just intelligent members, states Surowiecki. The different perspectives and skills brought by those seen as having less expertise will have a positive effect on the group. This, notes Surowiecki, represents a big shift in thinking for many businesses.

> **Suggesting that the organization with the smartest people may not be the best organization is heretical, particularly in a business world caught up in a ceaseless 'war for talent' and governed by the assumption that a few superstars can make the difference between an excellent and a mediocre company. Heretical or not, it's the truth: the value of expertise is, in many contexts, overrated.**

The more diverse a group, the more independent its members are likely to be. Homogeneity makes people likely to go along with the opinions of others, even if they disagree. Without independence of opinion, the group loses its ability to get things right.

That's why independence is the second condition of a group's ability to produce good decisions. In this instance, independence just means that each member of the group isn't dependent on any other member for information. Surowiecki points out that people can still be biased and irrational, as long as they're not under the influence of others.

He says: 'the more influence we exert on each other, the more likely it is that we will believe the same things and make the same mistakes. This means it's possible we could become individually smarter but collectively dumber.'

If the group is the people that make up a business, it's obvious that all members will spend a lot of time interacting with each other. But the negative effects of this can be minimized (in decision-making terms) by ensuring as much as possible that people make their decisions simultaneously, and are therefore less likely to follow each other into bad ones. In fact, businesses themselves must ensure they don't make the same mistake, and follow other organizations into making bad decisions. This is harder than it sounds, because the reasoning behind doing this – that the examples set by others are worth following – is rational. But the more people who get on the bandwagon, the more obvious it is that the decisions aren't made by the group at all, but, more probably, by one influential individual (or organization); the rest are following. Surowiecki calls these sequences in which bad decisions are copied 'information cascades'. If there's one positive angle of an information cascade, from a business point of view, it's that occasionally a business, product or service suddenly becomes the focus of one and therefore benefits.

What's needed, from an organization's point of view, to minimize this effect, is a method of ensuring all members of the group are decentralized – i.e. they can draw on local and specialized knowledge – and that their decisions or solutions are aggregated.

The concept of an aggregator is a very important one. In fact, without a method of aggregation, the wisdom of crowds wouldn't be a workable concept at all. In a business, it's possible the CEO, the senior management team, or the board could put themselves in the role of an aggregator, collecting and analyzing the independent and decentralized decisions of the company's departments (or the group's members). The method of aggregation is largely irrelevant, though Surowiecki shows how internal decision markets can be used to great effect to inform decisions.

There are many traps a business can fall into, according to Surowiecki. It's not the case, for example, that the best decision a crowd can come up with would be a consensus. This is the opposite of those myriad of independent, individual decisions that are then aggregated. The search for consensus 'encourages tepid, lowest-common-denominator solutions which offend no-one rather than exciting everyone'. It can also discourage employees from expressing dissent or carrying out independent analysis.

Additionally, businesses must ensure that all the power isn't concentrated at the top, with endless layers of hierarchy beneath. Instead, a (decentralized) culture should be cultivated whereby those local to a problem should be those solving it, and employees and managers are empowered to make decisions and to look for ways to improve operations. This will create engaged employees who can be relied on to improve the business, leaving senior managers freer to focus on other things. The danger is that employees become more loyal to their department or division than to the company as a whole, and this needs to be avoided. The most drastic case of this danger of employees working in competition with each other is identified by Surowiecki as Enron. 'Decentralization only works if everyone is playing on the same team,' he says.

To increase employees' engagement further, and incentivize them into being active and interested members of the group, evidence points to stock options making a big difference, with one study finding that when the majority of employees own stock options, the company sees improvements in corporate productivity, profits, and stock market returns. But greater decision-making power among employees will be most effective when improving the company's performance.

Running through *The Wisdom of Crowds* is a warning that for a business to harness this wisdom, the CEO cannot be treated like a superhero. In fact, the belief that the right individual at the top is the key to corporate success doesn't hold true, and Surowiecki shows that there's little evidence that an individual can consistently make better decisions or forecasts than the group. (The fact that two-thirds of all mergers end up destroying shareholder value proves CEOs are not extraordinary decision makers, he says.)

How real companies use Surowiecki's concepts

Surowiecki identifies three types of problem: cognitive, coordination and cooperation. Coordination problems are often very important to an organization – who will work where? How much should my factory produce? How can we make sure people get the goods and services they want? A company that uses the wisdom of crowds to good effect when it comes to coordination is fashion retailer Zara, according to Surowiecki. It may seem surprising that Zara doesn't outsource most of its design or manufacturing, but the company has brought it all in-house, to effectively make its suppliers its partners. This allows Zara to coordinate the actions of its employees to achieve its goal of staying up to date by producing new ranges quickly. The effect of this is to coordinate the group's (the business's) behavior with the desire of its customers. Surowiecki explains:

> **The general rule … is that companies will do things for themselves when it is cheaper and easier than letting someone else do them. But it's also the case that companies will do things for themselves if they are so important that it's not worth the risk of letting someone else do them. For Zara, speed and control are more important than sheer cost.**

The types of problems that are most amenable to collective decision making are, Surowiecki suggests, cognition problems. These define corporate strategy and tactics, being concerned with everything from deciding which product to launch to setting processes or forecasting demand. Surowiecki identifies General Electric and General Motors as early examples of companies which tried to harness the collective thoughts and ideas of the group. 'It's telling that the two most respected CEOs of the twentieth century – Alfred Sloan of General Motors and Jack Welch of General Electric – were both ardent advocates of a more collective approach to management.' Sloan encouraged ideas from employees at all levels within the company, taking what he called a 'decentralized approach' (presumably in which he and his management team fulfilled the aggregation function), and Welch reduced the layers of management and hierarchy within GE in an effort to create a 'boundaryless corporation'.

Surowiecki also points out that Google's entire model is based on tapping into the wisdom of crowds. In effect, Google is the aggregator. In a 2004 article in *Forbes Magazine*, Surowiecki said, 'The most valuable resource on the Internet is the collective intelligence of everyone who uses it.' He explains that Google's PageRank algorithm essentially asks web page producers to vote on which other web pages are most worthwhile, with each link acting as a vote.

How it dovetails with other guru theories

Four years before *The Wisdom of Crowds* was published, Malcolm Gladwell's *The Tipping Point* was released to huge acclaim, and focused heavily on how members of a group can influence one another. *The Tipping Point* posits that it's possible to influence a trend which reaches a moment of critical mass that triggers a social epidemic. Ideas can spread like viruses. The aim of the book is to show people how to start positive epidemics of their own. *The Tipping Point* then describes what happens when crowds aren't wise, and how to harness ensuing 'information cascades', as Surowiecki would refer to them, to your own advantage.

Validity today

The Wisdom of Crowds was only published in 2004, so it has not yet had to survive the test of time. However, the role of the internet and social media has come to the forefront of operations for many businesses and is something not really touched on by Surowiecki. The phenomenon of crowdsourcing (a term coined by the *Wired* journalist Jeff Howe in his article 'The Rise of the Crowdsourcing') is built on the wisdom of crowds and the internet makes tapping into this much easier. The concept of asking a diverse group of strangers for ideas or solutions has become more familiar to businesses. Having some way of aggregating what people are saying on the internet − Twitter is the most obvious example − on a particular topic may be one way of using the wisdom of crowds to forecast or to find solutions.

The difficulty, though, may come with ensuring Surowiecki's criteria are all met. Diversity might be assumed, and aggregation may be possible, but anybody hoping to harness this wisdom would also have to ensure respondents aren't being influenced by the answers, forecasts or solutions that others are providing.

Businesses looking to the internet should therefore be mindful of the drawbacks and use the answers to inform, rather than dictate. The pace of change is boggling, though, and new ways of asking for and aggregating crowd contributions are springing up continually.

Sun-Tzu

By Modwenna Rees-Mogg

Name: Sun-Tzu

Born: 544 BC

Expertise: Listing all the rules of combat that are necessary to win a war, without conflict

Known for: Having inspired everyone from famous war generals to business leaders, politicians and sports stars in how to use the right tactics and psychology to win an objective by outwitting the enemy/competition.

Best-known title: *The Art of War*

Who is Sun-Tzu?

Sun-Tzu lived during the Warring States period after the Zhou dynasty. It's believed that he served under King Helü of Wu. There are myriad tales of *The Art of War* being a key text used by warriors throughout history. In the West, generals from Napoleon to Colin Powell are reported to have been profoundly influenced by it. In the East, it is said to have influenced Chairman Mao.

What Sun-Tzu is known for?

Since the evolution of business management theory, *The Art of War* has been and continues to be integral to academic thought and business application, as it contains dozens of perfectly synthesized quotes about how to achieve strategic objectives. *The Art of War* is not about winning at all cost or going to war; it is about making winning pay by using the ingenuity of the human mind to develop tactics and strategies to achieve the outcome required.

It is said that King Helü ordered Sun-Tzu to train 180 of his concubines to become soldiers. Sun-Tzu divided them into two companies, putting each of the King's two favorite concubines in charge. When he ordered them to face right, they giggled. Sun-Tzu explained to them that they must obey the general's (i.e. his) orders. They giggled again. Despite the King's protests, Sun-Tzu ordered the execution of the two favorites and appointed two others to replace them as leaders.

Afterwards both companies performed their maneuvers without making any mistakes. His reasoning was that if the general's soldiers understood the orders, but disobeyed, then it was the fault of the officers. Once a King had given an order, it was the duty of the general to carry it out, even if the King later protested.

The concepts

According to Sun-Tzu, winning a war is all about pursuing a distinct strategy based on 13 key themes.

1. Making of plans

Sun-Tzu emphasizes that war is a serious thing and, to be won, everything must be planned, including the setting of objectives, planning the resources needed to achieve the outcomes, building the right team, understanding the strengths and weaknesses of the opposition, preparing for the unexpected and, last but not least, the attack. Victory is measured in simple terms: most spells victory; least spells defeat; none, surer defeat.

2. Waging of war

He was clear that a war should be waged quickly or it would sap the energy, resources and morale of both the army and the country from which the army has come. By understanding the damage war can do, a good general can work out the most profitable way of conducting it. Armies must be managed very efficiently, e.g. he said that armies should forage off the enemy in order to preserve food and other resources being brought up through the supply chain.

3. Strategic offensive

The view of Sun-Tzu was that the skillful strategist 'defeats the enemy without doing battle'. He believed that a target of whatever size should be captured intact rather than defeated, and that a long siege was the lowest form of war. He was opposed to interference and meddling by ignorant people and felt that leaders and troops should have aligned objectives. Everyone should be prepared for the unexpected and therefore should know the enemy and what it may be planning.

4. Forms and dispositions

Warriors should aim to become invulnerable by really knowing themselves and what they are planning, not by dreaming. They should exploit the enemy's vulnerabilities. Victory should be inevitable and only happens when there are no slip-ups on any chance of defeating the enemy. Victory is not the same as doing battle. In a war, victory is achieved only after measurement, estimation, calculation and comparison have been achieved.

5. Potential energy

Sun-Tzu said that management is all about the correct division of resources. Indirect warfare is preferable to direct warfare and should be unending until victory is achieved, but can be mixed in an infinite number of ways with direct warfare. Timing is all and, in order to achieve victory, the energy used by the army must be focused, but unending until the finish; disorder is disastrous. An important skill is to tempt the enemy into declaring itself and then move with full force against him.

6. Empty and full

A skillful warrior lures his enemy into a trap and then exhausts him. Part of the tactics of destroying an enemy is to unsettle him, in whatever appropriate way you can. It is better to go to a place where there is no enemy, than to confront him in battle. Attack the undefended if you can, but always defend your own vulnerable spots. Swift movement to confuse the enemy is as important as keeping him unaware of your plans. No successful victory is ever quite like another, so a warrior needs to remain very responsive to changing situations.

7. The fray

If you do battle, throw all your resources into it. Speed is the essence of attack; make sure you have your rearguard covered. Exploit every piece of information you have to turn the battle your way. Scare your enemies by making yourself appear larger than you are. Time your attacks for when the enemy is most vulnerable; do not attack when you cannot win. Treat the enemy with great respect, even after you have won.

8. The nine changes

Do not put yourself into a weakened position. Do not take roads that are unsuitable just to try to achieve a victory; nor attack enemies that you cannot beat. Form alliances if necessary. If you need to, fight to the death. Always balance opportunities against threats. Keep the enemy weak by making them wonder what you are going to do next. Avoid recklessness, cowardice, a hot temper, a delicacy of honor and undue concern for the individual as opposed to the army as a whole.

9. On the march

If you have to confront the enemy directly, protect your own position as much as possible, using everything you have. In particular, consider your terrain and adapt yourself to take advantage of any cover it may provide. Retreat from dangerous positions immediately; let the enemy enter them. Some terrains are rich with ready traps, so be particularly careful here. Learn and look out for signs of trouble and for clues to help you understand what the enemy is doing. Never underestimate the enemy. Sun-Tzu emphasized that a good general is not tyrannical and, having trained his troops well, commands them with civility and discipline. Building mutual trust is everything.

10. Forms of terrain

Sun-Tzu believed that if you studied terrain you could then execute the best battle strategy; therefore a wise general studies how to react on different terrains and fully trains his troops in this context, long before going to war. He said that if you know your enemy and you know yourself, you will always achieve a victory.

11. The nine kinds of ground

There are different ways of dealing with each type of ground you may encounter. Keep your own army on the move and challenge them to achieve the seemingly impossible. Do not give them an easy way out and put them in situations where they all win by helping each other. Never allow them to get superstitious. Leaders must remain all knowing, inscrutable, upright and impartial, and above all make sure the enemy never knows what they are going to do next. Lead from the front, but keep everyone together behind you. Do not explain dangers to your troops, but show the advantages of the strategy adopted.

When you do decide to attack, close off every escape route and firmly execute your plans; and act swiftly.

12. Attack by fire

There are always better times to attack than others, but when you do, you must destroy whatever is in your sights. Always attack from afar, if you can, and position yourself so that you cannot be burned by the fires you have started. Never start an attack through anger or spite; only do it if it is to your advantage. Don't burn your boats. Sun-Tzu believed above all that the enlightened ruler is prudent and the effective general is cautious. If these two individuals follow these beliefs, a nation will remain at peace and an army intact.

13. Espionage

Sun-Tzu believed in the incredible power of spies and in spending well to get the information you need from them, as it is cheaper than going to war. You need people on your side who understand how the enemy thinks. This information is far more important than using assumptions gained from guesswork or theoretical calculation. Spies must be kept closest of all to the general and should be the most highly rewarded people in the army. Spies must be treated wisely, with humanity and justice, but you need to treat what they tell you with care. Destroy those spies who divulge your information and those to whom they have told it, but if you capture an enemy spy, you should turn him into a double agent and treat him generously.

In Sun-Tzu's view, fighting was expensive and should be avoided if possible; winning is about preserving your resources and keeping costs low. Enemies create opportunities. Success will create more enemies, not fewer. He also showed us that there is science in war; it is not a simple art.

How real companies use Sun-Tzu's concepts

Almost every business in the world will be applying some or all of Sun-Tzu's concepts, either knowingly or unknowingly, from the day they first write a business plan. There are even specific training companies that have been used by global corporates across the world to train their staff in doing business according to *The Art of War*.

There are as many instances of when a company has gone to war and won (e.g. Microsoft's battle with Netscape) as there are of when it has gone to war and lost (e.g. BA's battle with Virgin) but this only goes to prove Sun-Tzu's view that one battle does not a victory make. Meanwhile, undermining the enemy in order to achieve victory without actually resorting to war remains a popular tactic in business. A good example of this is the way companies such as the UK supermarket chains use television advertising to show how their products are cheaper, fresher or more relevant to their customers than those of their competitors. Ensuring that you remain the first among equals in your market, by having an ever-improving offering (e.g. Google) is also a strategy of which Sun-Tzu would have approved.

How it dovetails with other guru theories

Sun-Tzu is perhaps the founder of modern business thought, two thousand years before this school of study was even conceived. The themes behind his rules have been replicated by gurus, whether acknowledged or unacknowledged, ever since.

However, *The Art of War* has directly spawned a variety of business books in the last 20 years, including *Sun Tzu The Art of War for Executives*, Donald G Krause (1995); *The Complete Sun Tzu for Business Success: Use the Classic Rules of the Art of War to Win the Battle for Customers and Conquer the Competition*, Gerald A Michaelson and Steven W Michaelson (November 2011); and *Doing Business in China: Sun Tzu's 'The Art of War' as a Means of Understanding How the Chinese Do Business*, Laurence J Brahm (2004).

Validity today

Many of the themes in *The Art of War* are as valid today in the business world as they were in the warring period during Sun-Tzu's life.

Some are surprisingly modern, especially his comments on planning, tactics and the way to treat and lead teams of people. Perhaps one that is outdated is his view that a general should act on the first orders of his ruler, even if the ruler then changes his mind; a view today's active investors would certainly oppose.